Catholic Handbook

Essentials for the 21st Century

Explanations, Definitions, Prompts, Prayers, and Examples

WILLIAM C. GRAHAM

Paulist Press
New York/Mahwah, NJ

Nihil obstat: Rev. Donald E. Blumenfeld, Ph.D.
Archdiocese of Newark
Censor Librorum
May 28, 2009

Imprimatur: +Most Reverend John J. Myers, D.D., J.C.D.
Archbishop of Newark
June 9, 2009

The Imprimatur is an official declaration that a book or pamphlet is free of doctrinal or moral error. No implication is contained therein that those who have granted the Imprimatur agree with the contents, opinions or statements expressed.

Cover and book design by Lynn Else

Library of Congress Cataloging-in-Publication Data

Graham, William C., 1950–
    A Catholic handbook : essentials for the 21st century : explanations, definitions, prompts, prayers, and examples / William C. Graham.
        p. cm.
    Includes bibliographical references.
    ISBN 978-0-8091-4639-0 (alk. paper)
    1. Catholic Church—Handbooks, manuals, etc. I. Title.
    BX842.G73 2010
    297—dc22

                                                        2009039698

Published by Paulist Press
997 Macarthur Boulevard
Mahwah, New Jersey 07430

www.paulistpress.com

Printed and bound in the
United States of America

CONTENTS

ACKNOWLEDGMENTS

I am grateful to all who, in any way and many ways, have contributed to getting this little book into print:

Paul McMahon of Paulist Press first suggested the idea and encouraged me each step of the way; Dr. Nancy de Flon of Paulist Press carefully edited the final copy with attentiveness, efficiency, and grace.

Bishop Donald Kettler and his household at Kobuk House in the Diocese of Fairbanks provided space, hospitality, and good company as I wrestled with the manuscript.

My students at the College of St. Scholastica, by their perceptive questions and comments, helped shape both questions and answers; Lori Barnstorf of the College of St. Scholastica was kind and patient as she offered assistance in any number of ways.

This book is dedicated to my four sisters:

Sherry,
Luanne,
Gloria, and
Julie.

To all who assisted, I am happy to offer thanks. Any shortcomings in this text, however, are my responsibility alone.

What has been is what will be,
and what has been done is what will be done;
and there is nothing new under the sun.
• *Ecclesiastes 1:9*

And the one who sat upon the throne said,
"Behold, I make all things new."
• *Revelation 21:5*

While Paul was so speaking in his defense,
Festus said in a loud voice,
"You are mad, Paul; much learning is driving you mad."
• *Acts 26:24*

PREFACE

In over two millennia, Vatican II notes, the Church has never failed to come together to celebrate the paschal mystery, giving thanks to God for the inexpressible gift of Christ Jesus, in praise of God's glory through the power of the Holy Spirit. Considering this unbroken stream of praise and thanksgiving, one feels either astonishment or wonder and, certainly, hope.

In coming together in praise of God, the Church first tells the story of the wonders God has done. Feasts follow stories; thus the Christian year moves from festival to festival. After the telling of the story and subsequent celebrations, theology follows: words (*logos*) about God (*Theos*) seeking to make sense of what has been revealed. Consider that the eleventh-century monk Boso said to Anselm, the great theologian and archbishop of Canterbury, "It appears a neglect if, after we are established in the faith, we do not seek to understand what we believe." So for over two thousand years, Christians have celebrated in thanksgiving for the gift of life from God in the person of Christ through the activity of the Holy Spirit. Artists, storytellers, party givers and goers, pastors, and theologians, too, all stand under the mystery, seeking somehow to consider and convey what is ineffable, beyond our ability either to understand or to express.

Those who have questions about the tradition stand revealed as seekers on pilgrimage to God. Questions and even doubts can be holy, for they prompt us to continue the journey, seeking the truth. When we find that truth, we will be face to face with Christ, in whom is all our delight.

My hope is that these questions will prompt further discussion and more questions. I invite readers who wish to continue the dialogue to send along questions that could be gathered into a future volume. Questions with CATHOLIC HANDBOOK in the subject line can be sent to me at WCGNYCPL@aol.com.

Now let the quest continue that the prize may be had!

William C. Graham
July 29, 2008
Kobuk House in Fairbanks, Alaska

I

THE BIG PICTURE
Structure, Governance, and Issues

The goal set before us is no trifling one;
We are striving for eternal life.

—St. Cyril of Jerusalem
from a catechetical instruction

THE COMMUNION OF SAINTS

I heard a voice from heaven say,
"Write this: Blessed are the dead who die in the Lord from
*   now on."*
"Yes," said the Spirit, "let them find rest from their labors,
for their works accompany them."

—Revelation 14:13

To live above with the Saints we love,
*   ah, that is the purest glory;*
to live below with the saints we know,
*   ah, that is another story.*

—Irish folk wisdom

The hymn "For All the Saints," by William Walsham How (1823–97), suggests the union of the Church below with the saints triumphant above:

1

O blest communion, fellowship divine!
We feebly struggle, they in glory shine;
Yet all are one in thee, and all are thine.
Alleluia, Alleluia!

The vision in this hymn suggests one Church in which
are united the people of God both on earth and in heaven. We
see the task of the Church, then, as one of transformation:
individuals are clothed in Christ and become sisters and
brothers, one of another and of Christ, adopted sons and
daughters of the most high God, called together by the Spirit
to be the Body of Christ. Each Christian is told author-
itatively in the baptismal ceremony: "You have become a new
creation; you have clothed yourself in Christ."

The final stanza of another hymn, "Thou, who at Thy
first Eucharist didst pray" by William Harry Turton (1856–
1938), sees the unity of the Church on earth with the
Church gathered around the throne of God:

So, Lord, at length when sacraments shall cease,
May we be one with all your Church above,
One with your saints in one unending peace,
One with your saints in one unbounded love.

This vision is also seen in the book *The Imitation of
Christ* by Thomas à Kempis (b. 1379 or 1380, d. 1471).
When that which is perfect comes, sacraments will cease;
the blessed in heaven's glory have no need of sacramental
remedy. The Church's vision calls us both to hope and to
endurance as we wait in joyful hope for the second coming
of Christ.

THE NICENE CREED

Creed comes from the Latin word *credo*, "I believe." A creed, then, is a statement of what the Church believes, those truths that bind the members together. The Nicene Creed was written by the Council of Nicaea in 325 and amplified by the Council of Constantinople in 381. This profession of the Christian faith is used not just by the Catholic Church, but by the Eastern Churches separated from Rome, and by most Protestant denominations:

> We believe in one God,
> the Father, the Almighty,
> maker of heaven and earth,
> of all that is, seen and unseen.
> We believe in one Lord, Jesus Christ,
> the only Son of God,
> eternally begotten of the Father,
> God from God, light from light,
> true God from true God,
> begotten, not made, one in Being with the Father.
> Through him all things were made.
> For us men and for our salvation
> he came down from heaven:
> by the power of the Holy Spirit he was born of the
>   Virgin Mary, and became man.
> For our sake he was crucified under Pontius Pilate;
> he suffered, died, and was buried.
> On the third day he rose again
> in fulfillment of the Scriptures;
> he ascended into heaven
> and is seated at the right hand of the Father.

He will come again in glory to judge the living and
the dead,
and his kingdom will have no end.
We believe in the Holy Spirit, the Lord, the giver
of life,
who proceeds from the Father and the Son.
With the Father and the Son he is worshiped and
glorified.
He has spoken through the Prophets.
We believe in one holy catholic and apostolic Church.
We acknowledge one baptism for the forgiveness of
sins.
We look for the resurrection of the dead,
and the life of the world to come. Amen.

IS THERE A DIFFERENCE BETWEEN RELIGION AND SPIRITUALITY?

We have in our age some confusion between religion,
religious practice, and spirituality. In exploring spirituality,
a person seeks something greater than her- or himself. This
experience might include religious awe or reverence; it
might also include religious practice. Some see spirituality as
a private affair as it seeks good psychological health, often
focusing on personal experience.

Our various religions and Christian denominations are
spiritualities. For example, John Wesley was an Anglican
priest in the Church of England who believed that Christians could become perfect in this life; they did not have to
wait for eternal life. He had a Method, or a Spirituality,
which earned him the derision of his fellow clergy. They
made fun of John Wesley and his little Method and of his
Method-ist followers. But he bravely called those followers

into a reformed church to do not only works of piety, but works of mercy. These works, he believed, would put Christians on the path to perfection in love.

Religion is not a solitary affair but calls together a community of seekers. The word *religion* means to be bound together in relationship or betrothed as lovers committed to each other. The human quest for meaning is never done in isolation. It is in community that life's meaning and values are communicated to the religious community's newcomers. Institutions and religions grow up from these needs. Christians are reminded that Jesus did not address a collection of individuals but rather Israel; those who are baptized are joined individually to God by becoming members of the Body of Christ, in which they are joined one to another as sisters and brothers.

STRUCTURE: DIOCESE AND PARISH, BISHOP AND PRIEST

The Catholic Church throughout the world is divided into regions known as dioceses. Each diocese or particular church is entrusted to the local bishop who works in cooperation with his group of priests. Each diocese is divided into parishes.

The *Code of Canon Law* emphasizes that the diocesan bishop is bound to propose and explain to the faithful the truths of the faith so that Christian doctrine is handed on to all (#386 §1).* Further, he is to show an example of holiness in charity, humility, and simplicity of life, while striving to

---

*The Code of Canon Law is numbered throughout for easy reference by paragraph (#) and by sentence §. So the reference above #386 §1 means paragraph 386 of the Canon, sentence 1 of that paragraph.

promote in every way the holiness of the Christian faithful according to the proper vocation of each (Can #387).

A parish is a certain community of the Christian faithful whose pastoral care is entrusted to a pastor by the authority of the diocesan bishop. Church law obliges a pastor to proclaim the word of God to those living in the parish, instructing the Christian faithful in the faith, especially by preaching on Sundays. Further, he is to foster works that promote the spirit of the gospel and social justice (Can #528 §1). The Eucharist is the heart both of the universal Church and of the parish, binding together all those who participate.

Church law also stipulates that a pastoral council should be established in each parish to assist in fostering pastoral activity. This council has a consultative vote and is governed by the norms established by the diocesan bishop (Can #536 §1, §2). Each parish is to have a finance council to assist the pastor in the administration of the goods of the parish (Can #537). Some pastors have associate pastors or parochial vicars, priests who share the pastor's duties in caring for a parish. Additionally, many parishes employ a variety of lay ecclesial ministers or members of religious congregations to assist in many ministries.

WHAT ARE MY RIGHTS AND DUTIES AS A CATHOLIC ?

Christians are equally sons and daughters of the most high God, brothers and sisters together in the Body of Christ, with Christ as the Head of the Church. By virtue of their baptism, they share in the task of building up the Body of Christ, each in her or his own way. Each is to fulfill the duties common to every member of the Church. Every member is called to holiness and has both the duty and the right to work to bring the good news to every land and heart (see Can #208–11).

Church members have the freedom to inform their pastors of their needs and desires. Further, the law stipulates that the knowledge, competence, and prestige of local church members bring the right and sometimes the duty to make known to pastors their opinions on matters pertaining to the good of the Church. Sometimes these church members must also make their opinions known to others among the faithful, attentive always to the dignity of all involved (Can #212 §2, §3).

Catholics have a right to the sacraments (Can #213). This is a very significant point: Sacramental nourishment is not a privilege that the hierarchy makes available out of kindness or charity. Rather, since the Church makes the Eucharist and the Eucharist makes the Church, it is essential to remember that sacramental activity is God's gift to be shared among the people of God.

Called by baptism to lead a life in keeping with the gospel, the faithful have the right to a Christian education, as they strive both to mature and to live the mystery of salvation (Can #217). Scholars are cheered and challenged to note that they enjoy freedom of inquiry and freedom of expressing their opinion on those matters in which they possess expertise (Can #218).

All the Christian faithful have the right to be free of coercion in choosing a state of life (Can #219). Nobody may harm another's good reputation or injure another's rights to protect his or her own privacy (Can #220). We can defend our rights, and we have the right to be judged according to the equitably applied law (Can #221 §1, §2).

We are obliged to assist with the needs of the Church so that the Church has what is necessary for worship, for works of the apostolate and of charity, and for decent support of ministers. We are further obliged to promote social justice and to assist the poor from our own resources (Can #222 §1, §2).

In exercising their rights, the Christian faithful, both as individuals and groups, are called to take into account the common good of the Church, the rights of others, and their own duties toward others (Can #223 §1).

LAY LEADERS OF WORSHIP

Some people are surprised to encounter lay leaders of community prayer. Lay ministry is not a new phenomenon; it is as old as the Church itself. There are instances in which the nonordained appropriately act as prayer leaders and in which they claim their rightful place among the people of God. For example, it is entirely usual that morning or evening prayer be led by one of the participants, who might also reflect on the proclaimed Scripture.

A layperson may lead at a wake or even at a funeral when a priest or deacon is unavailable. They also visit the sick and bring communion to them. Sometimes, a layperson may lead at a Sunday service in the absence of a priest. There is a ritual provided for such a service, but it is and should be a rare occurrence. Such a circumstance will legitimately provoke the lament, "Wouldn't it be nice to have a priest?"

Lay ministers ought to expect to be welcomed by the praying community. Sometimes and sadly, however, lay leaders will find their ministry questioned, objected to, and even openly opposed. But we who live in this extraordinarily well-educated Church are coming more and more to recognize the ministries of those who serve us outside of holy orders.

FEASTS AND SEASONS

Josef Jungmann, a Jesuit professor of liturgy at Innsbruck in the 1800s, was of the opinion that the most effective way to preach the faith is to celebrate a feast. Christians celebrate feasts and tell stories; out of these activities, theology and the liturgical year grow. In the *General Norms for the Liturgical Year and the Calendar*, we are reminded that the yearly cycle celebrates the whole mystery of Christ (*GNLY* #17). We are further reminded of Sunday's rank as the first holy day of all (*GNLY* #4).

The *Constitution on the Sacred Liturgy*, a document from the Second Vatican Council, notes that in the course of the year, the Church unfolds the mystery of Christ from the incarnation and nativity, through the paschal mystery, to the ascension and to Pentecost, all in the hope of the second coming of Christ (#102). So Sunday by Sunday and year by year, we celebrate the paschal mystery, beginning with Advent and ending with the feast of Christ the King.

LIBERAL OR CONSERVATIVE?

There are rigorists among us and some who are more lax in their practice. Often, they charge one another as inside or out of *orthopraxis* (correct practice). Some sometimes accuse another of being a "cafeteria Catholic," one who decides herself which rules and laws apply. In the midst of such confusion and occasional mean-spiritedness, our call is to learn to appreciate one another's contributions to Church and community, remembering always the command of Jesus: "Stop judging, that you may not be judged" (Matt 7:1).

There are fearful and angry souls who remain within the Roman Church but who, in their outrage, seem to forget the promise of Christ to Peter that "on this rock I will build my church, and the gates of the netherworld will not prevail against it" (Matt 16:18). We cannot forget or rework the words of Jesus. We cannot suggest that we know better than the Messiah or the Spirit. Our own opinions are not on par with revelation, and sometimes opinions emit a suspicious smell.

We must find the common ground that the late Joseph Cardinal Bernardin encouraged us to seek: There, in that shared spot, is the table from the upper room, the cross of Christ, the empty tomb, the road to Emmaus, the flame of Pentecost; there, Christ presides. While previous generations disputed with those they termed "the separated brethren," and today greet them with the dignity and respect they are owed, many Catholics sometimes seem to engage one another in warfare, which is not helpful to the Church or any individual member. Those who see themselves as conservative seem to suggest that no conversation is necessary since they have both pope and truth in their corner. Others, characterized as liberals, are often ready for dialogue, thinking that when the opposing camp listens long enough, they will at last be converted. Together both camps need to seek the truth that liberates, and the "truth will set you free" (John 8:32).

WHO CAN GO TO HEAVEN?

Can Protestants go to heaven? To begin to answer that question, look at a recent address by Pope Benedict XVI to pilgrims in St. Peter's Square. He said, "The missionary role is shared by all baptized people who are all called to be bearers of the message of peace." He also commented on the meaning of the missionary mandate for each believer, affirming the Evangelist Luke's emphasis that the mission first given to the twelve apostles is not reserved to them, but extends to the disciples of every age; in God's field there is work for everyone, according to Benedict.

Additionally, in his message, Benedict XVI expressed his desire that the gospel reawaken in every baptized person an awareness of being a missionary of Christ, each called to prepare the way of the Lord, both in words and with the testimony of her or his life. That should get you to heaven.

What about Jews and Muslims, Buddhists and Hindus? Pope John Paul II noted in his book *Crossing the Threshold of Hope* that God can work outside the Church and outside the sacraments. This important observation is neither the pope's original insight nor late-breaking news. No one is outside God's saving power. The Church daily prays to God for all God's people who seek with sincere hearts (fourth Eucharistic Prayer). Do not all seekers look in sincerity for truth? For all of these, the Church prays day by day. And if someone could not be saved, what would be the point of praying for her or him? Speaking of other religious traditions, the Second Vatican Council (1962–65) also taught that the Catholic Church rejects nothing that is true or holy in other religions. Though their precepts or doctrines may differ significantly from Christian teaching, the Church has high regard for both conduct and the ways of life in other faiths in which is often reflected rays of the truth that enlighten all people (*Nostra Aetate* 2). This does not sound like the road to limbo, purgatory, or hell.

ARE PROTESTANT CHURCHES DEFECTIVE?

Pope John XXIII, who summoned the Second Vatican Council, noted that what separates believers in Christ—

Catholics from Protestants—is much less than what unites us. In a recent document that provoked heated discussion, Pope Benedict XVI notes that the Catholic Church is a visible and spiritual community in which, from its beginning and throughout the centuries, is found both apostolic succession and seven sacraments. He notes as well that there are other Christian communities that have not preserved the apostolic succession or a celebration of the Eucharist presided over by men ordained in this succession by a laying on of hands. He calls these communions "ecclesial communities." Benedict sees the divided Church as a wounded Church. Jesus prayed that the Church be one; divisions in the Christian family seem opposed to what he had in mind. Some consider it harsh to make any mention of the differences between Christian denominations. But assessing, discussing, and seeking to understand those differences will fulfill Vatican II's ecumenical intent and will stress that the Church remains committed to ecumenical dialogue.

Seeking to understand what makes us Catholic prompts us to take a historical view of what the reformers had in mind as they protested various abuses in the Church and questioned certain teachings, thus the name *Protestant*. They moved from the Roman communion to something new, a communion that viewed differently both apostolic succession and ministry through the laying on of hands. For Benedict to observe this as a distinguishing feature between Catholicism and other Christian communities or churches is not to denigrate them. Only when we understand our real differences can we truly appreciate diversity and hope to come to a new and better and full communion.

The Roman position is that the Church is a communion in Christ with apostolic succession through the laying on of hands and seven sacraments. If we Catholics lack that in any time or place, we are defective, we have omitted something essential. The reformers had different ideas; some do not see as essential either seven sacraments or apostolic succession through the laying on of hands. But only Methodists can say what constitutes the Methodist Church; so also for Presbyterians, Lutherans, and Baptists. The Vatican document *Dominus Iesus*, approved by then Cardinal Ratzinger, describes the Catholic communion, and what is essential to *us*. Protestants may and do protest that, and in freedom of conscience seek to follow Christ and live the gospel. Vatican II acknowledges that these ecclesial communions have certain of the elements of sanctification and truth, and for this reason, God may well use them as instruments of salvation.

We believers trust that our seeking will eventually bring us to see God face to face. It is justice rather than charity that prompts us to understand that other seekers, too, hope to see God. God alone will judge both them and us.

All Christians are called to follow the lead of St. Paul, trusting that "the one who began a good work in us will continue to complete it" (Phil 1:6). Until then, we can claim St. Thomas More's plea: "Pray for me, as I will for thee, that we may merrily meet in heaven."

WHAT'S THE STORY WITH PURGATORY?

The Church teaches that those who die in God's grace but who are imperfectly purified will undergo a final purification before entering the joy of heaven. Purgatory would seem then to be more of a process than a place. Since the Councils of Florence and Trent (in the fifteenth and sixteenth centuries), the Church has given the name purgatory to this final purification of the elect. Scripture sometimes speaks of cleansing fire, and the tradition of the Church is to pray for the dead. Both Scripture and Tradition then inform this particular teaching.

WHAT HAPPENS TO A CHILD WHO DIES BEFORE BAPTISM: DO WE "LIMBO" ANYMORE?

It is natural to wonder what happens to those who die without or before baptism. Since the time of St. Augustine (354–430), some have speculated that unbaptized infants are consigned to limbo, a pleasant place except that God is not there. (And how pleasant could that really be for one who seeks God?) *The Catechism of the Catholic Church* (#1261) points to the funeral rites for children who have died without baptism; the Church entrusts these children to the mercy of God, as it also does for children who die subsequent to baptism.

WHAT DOES THE CHURCH TEACH ABOUT SUICIDE?

Some people, both Catholics and those from other traditions, are sometimes distraught in thinking that those who commit suicide are sent to hell. The Church offers resources that are helpful and liberating in such conversations.

Before modern science helped us understand that suicide most often does not reflect despair in God's mercy but rather an unhealthy mind, suicide was considered unpardonable because one did not live to repent or confess. Those who died by suicide were often buried outside the Church and even outside the cemetery's physical gates. But note that

Church teaching in the *Catechism* (#2280–83) invites us to consider the effects of psychological disturbances, anguish, suffering, or torture on the one who commits suicide. Further, we are instructed that we should not despair of the eternal salvation of persons who have taken their own lives. By ways known to him alone, God will provide for those so afflicted. The Church prays for persons who have taken their own lives.

Consider the opening prayer of the funeral Mass, which articulates our hope:

> Almighty God, our Father,
> we firmly believe that your Son died and rose to life.
> We pray for our brother/sister [N.],
> who has died in Christ.
> Raise him/her at the last day
> to share the glory of the risen Christ,
> who lives and reigns with you
> and the Holy Spirit,
> one God, for ever and ever.

Now, funeral services for suicide victims are often held in Catholic churches and their bodies may be buried in consecrated graves. So our prayers, teachings, and practices should give us comfort. Finally, we have the words of Jesus: "Do not be afraid" (Matt 28:10). St. Paul reminds us: "Console one another with these words" (1 Thess 4:18).

II

THE LOCAL VIEW
Structures and Tools

Now I am beginning to be a disciple.
May nothing visible or invisible rob me of my prize, which
is Jesus Christ!

—St. Ignatius of Antioch
from a letter to the Romans

SHOULD I READ THE BIBLE? WHICH ONE?

Reading the Bible is a profitable activity. Some read it a few chapters a day from beginning to end; others read it a gospel or other book at a time. While there are many translations, the Bibles normally used by Catholics are those that include what we call the Deuterocanonical or Apocryphal books (certain books of the Old Testament that Protestants do not regard as inspired by God).

Catholics in the United States use *The New American Bible* in worship. The United States bishops provide a very helpful Web site on which one can find this entire Bible book by book, verse by verse (http://www.nccbuscc.org/nab /bible/index.htm); the Web site also provides the readings that are appointed each day for the celebration of the Eucharist (http://www.usccb.org/nab/index.shtml).

WHAT IS *LECTIO DIVINA*?

Lectio divina is Latin for spiritual (or divine) reading that calls the faithful into communion with God. While there are many fine spiritual books to guide and challenge those who seek to grow in holiness, the Scriptures are the place to begin as one seeks to study, ponder, listen to, and pray with God's word. One could begin with the site mentioned above, focusing on the Scripture readings appointed for daily Mass.

CATHOLIC SOCIAL TEACHING

These ten generally acknowledged principles highlight the major themes in recent Catholic social teaching:

1. *Dignity of the Human Person.* Because human life is sacred, and because all are made in the image and likeness of God, all people possess human dignity.
2. *Common Good and Community.* Relationships are fundamental in the Body of Christ, and human dignity and rights are realized in community. The Christian obligation to love our neighbor requires not just individual effort but social commitment as well. All people share the obligation to contribute to the common good.
3. *Option for the Poor.* Societies can be judged by how they treat the most vulnerable in their midst. Thus, public policy decisions must be made not in terms of "How can we be better off?" but rather in terms of "How will this decision affect the poor?" Jesus models this approach in the gospels, when he cares first for those who are oppressed or marginalized. Poverty wounds not just the poor but the entire community.

4. *Rights and Responsibilities.* If human dignity is to be protected in a healthy community, each person has a right to life and to those things human decency requires: food, shelter, clothing, employment, health-care, and education. Following these rights are duties and responsibilities: to one another, to families, and to the larger society.

5. *Role of Government and Subsidiarity.* The state works toward the moral good by promoting human dignity, protecting human rights, and seeking the common good. The participation of citizens is both a right and a responsibility so that governments can achieve these goals. Subsidiarity holds that the functions of government be performed at the lowest level possible: for example, the state should not do what can be carried out at the city level; the federal government should not perform what the state can do.

6. *Economic Justice.* The economy is to serve people; people do not serve the economy. Workers have a right to fair wages and safe conditions. They have a right to organize. One does not have a right to excessive wealth when others lack necessities. While competition and free markets are useful, it is the task of the state and of all society to ensure that needs that cannot be satisfied by the market system are met.

7. *Stewardship of God's Creation.* The earth and all it contains are gifts from God intended for use by all people. We are responsible for the earth and its goods as stewards, not just as consumers. Our respect for the earth is respect for God.

8. *Promotion of Peace and Disarmament.* Peace and justice are foundational to Catholic teaching. Pope Paul VI said, "If you want peace, work for justice."

9. *Participation.* All people share the right to participate in society's economic, political, and cultural life.
10. *Global Solidarity and Development.* The human family extends beyond the boundaries of nation, race, creed, economy, and ideas. All people are called to work globally for justice and the progress of peoples. This work must respect and promote personal, social, economic, and political rights, including the rights of nations and of peoples.

VOCATIONS

Christian people are called in baptism to bring the light of Christ to all the world. Those who hear and seek to answer that call do so from their own situations in life. The concept of vocation, then, is not so much what we do as how we go about our day-to-day lives. Those who are single or celibate, married or widowed, each have a place among God's people. One's vocation might be to raise children in a marriage, to seek a cure for cancer, to protect and serve the public in uniformed service. Priests and religious have vocations, but are not alone in hearing God's call to serve. One has a vocation if one declares or believes that one does. So, a bookstore clerk who seeks to serve customers kindly and efficiently may see her work as her vocation; a clerk working next to her may see his work simply as a job. One has a vocation; the other does not.

MONASTERIES AND RELIGIOUS LIFE

Some Christian people do not marry, but elect to follow God in a consecrated life, living in monasteries or other communities. Usually, they consecrate their lives through the profession of the evangelical counsels, most often vows of chastity, poverty, and obedience.

Today there are a great number of institutes of consecrated life in the Church, both for men and for women. Some keep to a strict cloister, living and praying within an enclosure of a monastery, while others have more active lives among the rest of the people of God. Each of these communities is called to be faithful to the mind and intent of the founder, to the spirit, character, and mission of their community, and to the traditions that bind the community together.

Consecrated life is neither clerical nor lay. Some communities are composed almost entirely of priests and are thus clerical. Others have been founded not to include those in holy orders. All institutes of consecrated life are dedicated in a special way to the service of God and of the whole Church. Any Catholic who has the required qualities can seek admittance into a monastery or other institute of consecrated life.

WHAT IS CONTEMPLATION?

In his book *The Springs of Contemplation: A Retreat at the Abbey of Gethsemani*, Thomas Merton, the much-revered Trappist monk wrote about a parish priest, aged about fifty, who came to the monastery, Kentucky's Gethsemani Abbey, from a small parish in a remote town in Texas. The priest expected a two-day crash course in becoming a contemplative, but, to his surprise, found himself alone. Merton asserted that the abbey guest house should be "for those who, open to be spoken with, want to be in silence."

The Texas priest realized right away that he could have simply stayed at home where he could be both silent and alone. Merton's point is that a quick course in contemplation is neither available nor even possible. He suggested that we must be clear about where we are and where we stand. Such a recognition is at the heart of a contemplative life. When one understands that the simple essentials are all one really needs, a peaceful contentment descends and God will take care of the rest. What causes us to suffer is to fall victim to the conviction that the action is somewhere other than where we are.

Silence, contemplation, and community are our open choices. Merton reported that, in community, he found Christ both present and at work. He knew that his intuition was correct because the people among whom he landed became his friends. He noted, though, that one feature of Christian community is finding ourselves among people we would not have selected had we been scouting for friends. This is a distinguishing characteristic of Church: we find ourselves surrounded by and immersed in a cast of characters rich in both grace and sin. Bound together in the family of the Body of Christ, we seek to see Christ at work, transforming us, our comrades, and our activities until the fullness of God's reign is unveiled.

As the pilgrims progress, silence can be either problem or grace. Merton noted that silence does not suggest absence, but rather a love so strong that we can be silent together. One thinks of the Quakers, silent together in God's good presence, and also of the eucharistic assembly silent together as the word and the mystery of Christ present among us are contemplated and celebrated. And, as Merton saw it, living both a contemplative and a disciplined life helps one to distinguish the real from the artificial. Recognizing what is artificial, one ought then see what is real.

That which is real will endure, and "whoever endures to the end will be saved" (Matt 10:22).

All the fruits of the Christian life that feed the virtue of endurance are not clearly visible on the day of enrollment in the catechumenate or the day of baptism, for then the adventure is just beginning. The Christian path, then, is the road to holiness through wholeness for those called to be people of peace, immersed in God's reign, striving at the invitation of Jesus to be perfected, as the heavenly Father is perfect (Matt 5:48). To have decided that this is where we stand and that here lies our hope means that we do not need more.

THE SEVEN PRECEPTS OF THE CHURCH

These seven obligations define the minimum effort of Church members for growing in love of God and neighbor:

1. To attend Mass on Sundays and holy days of obligation, and to rest from servile work on those days
2. To observe the days of abstinence and fasting
3. To confess our sins to a priest at least once a year
4. To receive the Eucharist at least once a year during the Easter season
5. To contribute to the support of the Church
6. To obey the marriage laws of the Church
7. To participate in the Church's mission of evangelization

THE CORPORAL ACTS OF MERCY AND THE SPIRITUAL ACTS OF MERCY

Because Jesus is merciful, so must the Church as the Body of Christ—and we as individual members of that

Body—be merciful. The Church has traditionally enumerated seven corporal and seven spiritual works of mercy.

The corporal works of mercy take their inspiration from Matthew 25:35–36:

- To feed the hungry
- To give drink to the thirsty
- To clothe the naked
- To shelter the homeless
- To visit the sick
- To visit the imprisoned
- To bury the dead

Also inspired by the gospels (see Mark 16:15; John 14:27; Luke 15:7, 6:27–28; Matt 6:12, 11:28; and John 17:24), the spiritual works of mercy are:

- To instruct the ignorant
- To counsel the doubtful
- To admonish sinners
- To bear wrongs patiently
- To forgive all offenses
- To comfort the sorrowful
- To pray for the living and the dead

WHAT ABOUT THE TRIDENTINE MASS AND PRAYING IN LATIN?

Catholics who grew up in the 1950s and early 1960s remember praying in Latin. The ritual had been set in place by the Council of Trent after the Protestant Reformation; that liturgy is popularly referred to as Tridentine. Altar boys learned the Latin responses to the prayers at the foot of the altar and the other parts proper to the altar server. Children's choirs were taught to sing the parts of the Mass, and most could pronounce Latin far better than they ever understood it.

Today, some parishes may celebrate Mass on Pentecost Sunday or some other days in the *lingua antiqua* and sing the Gregorian Chant's *Missa de Angelis* (Mass VIII), but afterward, even daily-Mass Catholics often say, "Well, that was a nice enough look at a museum piece, but I don't need to do that again." Still, the idea is that folks should know, or at least experience, that part of the tradition.

But even the most rigorously orthodox report succinctly and accurately: "It is nice to be in touch with our tradition and to experience the Mass as did our grandparents, but there was a layer of meaning entirely absent." The experience of praying, or attempting to pray, in Latin is a far better teacher than any explanation that might be offered.

Not all celebrations of the Mass in Latin, or with some parts sung in Latin, are the Tridentine Mass. The *novus ordo*, or the new order of the Mass since Vatican II, can be in any language, Latin or the vernacular. Tridentine refers to the form of the Mass in Latin that was modified by the Second Vatican Council. There are many issues involved in restoring the Tridentine liturgy. Some people suggest that they want to experience the joy of communion without the anguish of our modern-day differences. Others think that, because in the Tridentine Mass the priest has his back to the congregation and prays in a dead language, they will be spared homilies based on the priest's "Netflix queue." Won't happen! Even back in pre–Vatican II days, the homily or sermon was not in Latin.

The Church, in the wisdom of the ages, prompts us to pray in languages we understand. Those who sentimentalize another reality should not seek to impose it on others among the people of God.

HOW ABOUT SECULAR SONGS OR READINGS AT MASS?

The Church very capably selects scriptural readings for eucharistic celebrations that are appropriate for feasts and seasons as well as for particular celebrations such as weddings and funerals. Those who are moved by other writers, or those who find inspiration in popular music outside of hymnody, will usually not find their selections welcomed in the liturgy. These songs and writings can find other homes or venues, such as rehearsal dinners or wakes, where they may be both welcome and helpful. We should be encouraged by those who are inspired by St. Paul: "All things work for good for those who love God" (Romans 8:28). If they find inspiration in arts and letters, that inspiration can surely lead to God. Matters of taste should lead to helpful discussions and promote charity in dialogue.

III

SACRAMENTS
Faith, Religion, and Theology in Practice

Through the Spirit we acquire a likeness to God; indeed, we attain what is beyond our most sublime aspirations— we become God.

> —St. Basil the Great, bishop
> from the treatise *On the Holy Spirit*

WHAT IS RITUAL FOR?
OR, ARE WE REALLY WHAT WE EAT?

When a child is baptized, the parents and godparents receive a candle on the child's behalf kindled from the Easter candle. They are admonished that this light is entrusted to them to be kept burning brightly, and that the child, enlightened by Christ, is to walk always as a child of the light. With the flame of faith alive in his or her heart, the child can go out to meet the Lord when at last he comes.

What we are about in that ritual moment is well explained by the rite itself. We use the Latin *lex orandi, lex credendi* (the law of prayer establishes the law of belief) to suggest that the Church's prayer both explicates and shapes what the Church believes. For example, in the Preface for the Dedication of a Church (I), our prayer defines not just our holy space, but also our relationship as the Body of Christ to the house of the Church: The prayer asserts that in our house of prayer, God's presence is revealed by sacramental signs that unite us to God in the unseen bond of grace. God is at work in the Church, building a temple of living stones that will bring the Church to its full stature as the Body of Christ.

We, the living stones, are about transformation in grace, our own and that of all the world. St. Augustine, the great fifth-century theologian and bishop of Hippo, articulated that belief in calling the folks to communion. Showing the consecrated bread and wine to the people, he would say: "Behold what you are; become what you receive." The priest or deacon, in preparing the chalice, recalls that hope as he prays that the mystery of the water and wine may bring us to share the divinity of Christ who in humility shared our humanity.

Receptivity to and interaction with grace are concepts and opportunities that ought to give us pause, or Sabbath rest. The Church prays on Easter Sunday morning that our celebration raise us up and, by the Spirit who lives in us, renew our lives. The sacramental life of the Church renews and transforms us in just the ways that the prayers and outward symbols suggest: In baptism, we are washed, made clean, and incorporated into the Church. Confirmation confirms our baptism and endows us with the gifts of the Holy Spirit. The Prayer after Communion for the Twenty-seventh Sunday in Ordinary Time, literally translated from the original Latin, asks that we be saturated and nourished by the sacraments we have received, so that we may be transformed into that which we have consumed. The eucharistic celebration, then, suggests that we are or will become what we eat.

The sacrament of penance or reconciliation—in the confession of sins, laying on of hands, and pronouncement of absolution—brings both pardon and peace. The exchange of marriage vows unites a man and woman, who become cocreators with God, one in love for each other, with hearts, bodies, and minds open to the possibility of procreation. Holy orders sets men apart for sacred service.

Finally, the sacrament of the sick, in its prayers, laying on of hands, and anointing with oil, frees the sick person from sin and relieves and strengthens his or her soul, arousing great confidence in divine mercy.

CAN'T I PRAY ON THE GOLF COURSE OR FROM MY LA-Z-BOY RECLINER?

Consider Spike, who from time to time announces, "I don't go to church anymore. Not ever. Not even Christmas or Easter." He asks, "Can't I worship God from the golf course or from my La-Z-Boy recliner?" Simple answer: "Yes, Spike, you can pray anywhere, anytime. Even while you're smoking." But can Spike claim to be a Christian when his spiritual side is either hidden or private?

The *Didascalia Apostolorum*, a Church document from the third century, addresses that problem, which has apparently plagued the Church in every age. It says that no one should diminish the Church by her or his absence. The Body of Christ should not be diminished by even one member. We are not to tear apart the Body of Christ. Ouch!

Spike is a good man. He loves his wife, Wanda. He cares about and for his family. He does not defraud anyone in his business. He may love Jesus. Jesus, no doubt, loves him. But does Spike qualify as a good Christian or good Catholic? No. This religious business is a social affair. It is not about Spike at home in his La-Z-Boy recliner loving the Lord.

Now, it is conceivable that Spike might seek, craft, or practice a spirituality at home. But religion is not a solitary affair. If Spike still prays the Lord's Prayer, he asks of God, "Thy kingdom come, thy will be done." All who make that prayer are called together to be contributors to the unfolding reign of God; Christians work to do God's will and invite the fullness of God's kingdom when they seek to make of their churches a formative presence in the human community. Walter Rauschenbusch, the Baptist preacher and great prophet of the American Social Gospel early in the twentieth century, called Christians to work together, seeing the world as it is and fashioning it into the world as it ought to be.

Pastors today would call Spike and Wanda to be envelope holders and contributors on any number of levels and in any number of efforts. Today's Church will be smaller and poorer if Spike and Wanda are absent.

THE WHATS AND WHYS OF PRAYER, PRAISE, AND THANKSGIVING

The human heart feels itself pulled spontaneously to praise and thanksgiving, yet human need prompts much prayer in the form of petitions for favor, seeking God's intervention in both mundane affairs and matters perceived to be of life-and-death significance. The *Catechism of the Catholic Church* asserts that "transformation of the praying heart is the first response to our petition" (#2739). And, "since the heart of the Son seeks only what pleases the Father," a rhetorical question is posed, wondering "how could the prayer of the children of adoption be centered on the gifts rather than the giver?" (#2740).

A condition of the efficacy of prayer is that it be "resolutely united with that of Jesus" and then "we obtain all that we ask in his name" (#2741). We are reminded that "if we enter into the desire" of the Spirit of God, "we shall be heard." But two cautions are given, the first from the fourth-century monk and writer Evagrius Ponticus: "Do not be troubled if you do not immediately receive from God what you ask him; for he desires to do something even greater for you, while you cling to him in prayer." And from St. Augustine: "God wills that our desire should be exercised in prayer, that we may be able to receive what he is prepared to give" (#2737).

But are these prayers heard? The *Catechism* admonishes the questioner: "We ought to be astonished by this fact: when we praise God or give him thanks for his benefits in general, we are not particularly concerned whether our prayer is acceptable to him." However, "we demand to see the results of our petitions" (#2735).

The *Catechism* seems to concur with the great twentieth-century Jesuit theologian Karl Rahner, who writes in his book *On Prayer* that we are quick to judge our prayers of petition with regard to what we perceive as their efficacy. Those living in poverty, dying of starvation, being exploited as slaves, and being betrayed as women, and all others crushed by injustice, might well speak against prayers of petition. Rahner points to the wonderment of those in pain who philosophize about God's remoteness, asking if the one who set the world a-spin is now unaware of its humming. He concludes that "we are justified in being embittered by His silence."

But we continue to turn to God, lifting pleading hands in prayer, cherishing our faith that is unshaken, even in disappointment. Rahner suggests that those who denounce the value of the prayer of petition as vain and useless must be listened to seriously, but nevertheless, our faith in prayer is vital. He sees us suspended over the abyss of nothingness by the thread of God's mercy to which we cling with tenacity.

Rahner points out that we who can be contented with our lot and unmoved by the misfortunes of others cry out when disaster hits us. When our contentment rocks in the wind, we expect the blissfully ignored kingdom of heaven to make all things right immediately so that we can be happy, even while seeming to not need God nor search for the divine face. Perhaps we are in this sad state, he suggests, because we have yet to grasp God's glory in our midst: the cross on which hung our Savior. We miss the point that we suffer because we sin.

The evils from which we pray to be delivered, however, may not be evil at all when measured by God's standards. In fact, perhaps our prayer is not so much a genuine lifting of our sorrows to God, but rather a selfish whine in which we ask to have all adjusted to our selfish perception of need. Such prayer, which really seeks to press our wishes on God rather than abandon ourselves to his will, is more arrogance and rebellion than prayer.

But this is not to suggest that prayers of supplication are to be forsaken, because Christ taught us how to pray, and until the *parousia*, we see in Christ the answer and antidote to our accusations of the futility of prayer. It is Christ who teaches us to pray in supplication, confidence, and submission. Christ promises that all true prayer will be heard inasmuch as we seek to conform our own will to God's. Then, of course, we realize where we should have begun: that prayer transforms not God, but us who offer it.

We might attend to John Henry Newman, nineteenth-century Oxford don and convert who later became a cardinal. Newman points out in his sermons that we do not obtain salvation simply by wishing for it.

So, the one who prays in faith returns with a deepened awareness to the formulation of the *Catechism*, understanding that the first fruit of prayer is the transformation of the heart of the one who prays. Gifts may be given, healings may occur. God the all-powerful can and does work wonders in every age. But perhaps no wonder is so great as that transformation of the human heart from stone to flesh: pliant in awe before God's design, compliant with God's good will, eager to see how God's goodness and tender mercy allow both saints and sinners to cope with life's trials, and confident that God does not abandon those who cry out, but is attentive in loving-kindness.

KEEPING THE SABBATH ON SUNDAY

Since on the seventh day God was finished with the work he had been doing, he rested on the seventh day from all the work he had undertaken. So God blessed the seventh day and made it holy, because on it he rested from all the work he had done in creation.

—Genesis 2:1–3

The Sabbath is a weekly invitation to imitate God on day seven of creation. This Sabbath posture is not inactivity—it is true awe in the presence of majesty. God's own creative genius is the model. Genesis inspires us to recognize the handiwork of God with awe and wonder. In imitation and praise of the Creator, we reflect on and rejoice in the gifts that are ours to share. This rest, this true leisure, is an invitation to grace. But we are rarely able to participate in this kind of refreshing, rejuvenating activity while earning a living, attending to ledgers, managing accounts, and attending to families and the details of careers and obligations.

The Catechism of the Catholic Church makes clear reference to the issues involved in a proper observance of Sunday or a Sabbath rest, pointing out that God's action is the model for our own. We, too, ought to rest and be refreshed on the seventh day, and everyday work should be halted (#2172). Further, the *Catechism* notes the rhythm of work and rest, pointing to the Lord's Day as a help to everyone to enjoy adequate rest and leisure to cultivate family, cultural, social, and religious lives (#2184).

So, what ought to be the activities and attitudes that suggest proper attention to the mystery of the Sabbath? Again, the *Catechism* speaks clearly that Sunday should provide opportunity to worship, perform works of mercy, and relax both mind and body (#2185).

These are invitations to a reverential posture that imitates God's own pleasure in the wonderful work of the divine hand. Remember, the Spirit of God swept over the chaos as God called creation into being (Gen 1:2–3). As we are called to newness and fullness of life, that same Spirit who once hovered over the deep hovers still, assisting us to make a rich tapestry from the chaos of the strands of our lives. Sunday might then be viewed as the foretaste and promise of the paschal feast of heaven, a day to anticipate the "assembly of the firstborn enrolled in heaven" (Heb 12:23).

What should Sunday look like? In a culture more appreciative of multitasking than of being at true leisure, Sabbath rest can be seen as a revolutionary act, as revolutionary tranquility. We must be aware of the fact that our technological culture can enslave us unless we call a halt. Our Sunday activities should open our eyes to worship, real play, true joy, and honest simplicity, all of which reveal the Creator's genius.

Such Sabbath times call an intentional halt to some forms of activity to make room for other pursuits or heightened awareness, making room for poetry and other arts. St. Basil the Great (330–79) asserts that tranquility is the first step in our journey to sanctification. Theophane the Recluse (1815–94), a Russian Orthodox monk and saint, reminds us that we should not expect God's grace to act on its own; instead, that grace waits for us to decide to open our hearts and minds. We must open ourselves to experience what we already possess, for God's transforming gift plays about us and awaits our invitation to enter.

The simple truth is that to desire a Sabbath posture is the beginning of living that posture. The first part of the journey is the most difficult: wanting to come to this new life. Persevering with Sabbath attitudes and practices is not easy. But a firm will is sure to yield rich results.

Rabbi Abraham Joshua Heschel reminds us that, on the Sabbath, we especially care for the seed of eternity planted in the soul. He asserts that even thinking of business or labor should be avoided, for labor is a craft, but perfect rest is an art. Heschel looks to Exodus 35:3 and its prohibition against kindling home fires on the Sabbath day. He suggests that it is a double sin to show anger on the Sabbath, for the ancient rabbis interpreted the Exodus exhortation to mean that one must kindle no fire—not even the fire of righteous indignation.

The Sabbath path, then, is an invitation to those called to be people of peace to travel in gratitude the road to holiness through wholeness, to be immersed in God's reign, to strive at the invitation of Jesus to be perfected, as the heavenly Father is perfect (Matt 5:48). To decide that this is our posture is to live in such a way as to demonstrate that in the Sabbath is our hope. Do we need more?

CHRIST, THE SACRAMENT OF GOD

Pope St. Leo the Great, who reigned from 440 to 461, observed that whatever was visible in Christ has passed over into the sacraments. What was visible in Christ? Inclusion for the isolated, light for those in darkness, food for the hungry, drink for the thirsty, balm for the afflicted, healing for the sick, sight for the blind, and new life for the dead. His words and actions brought salvation to those who approached him in faith.

Christians see Jesus as the Christ, the Messiah, the Anointed One. In Christ, as the Christmas Preface to the Eucharistic Prayer says, we see our God made visible. In the sacraments, we encounter Christ. In Christ, we encounter God. Thus, in the words of the twentieth-century Dominican theologian Edward Schillebeeckx, we regard Christ as the Sacrament of the encounter with God.

WHAT IS THE DIFFERENCE BETWEEN SACRAMENTS AND SACRAMENTALS?

Sacramentals are objects blessed by the Church to provoke good thoughts and prayerful activity while increasing devotion to God. The Church teaches that the sacraments, seven of them, were instituted by Christ. Sacramentals, however, are established by the Church. They include, for example, such objects as holy water as a reminder of baptism, rosary beads, and statues. The number of sacramentals may well be unlimited.

INITIATION: BECOMING ONE IN THE BODY OF CHRIST

The Holy Spirit calls individuals to membership in the Body of Christ. We rise up from the baptismal pool reborn as children of God, members of the Body of Christ, one with the Church in seeking the fullness of the reign of God. Children born to Catholic parents are most often baptized shortly after birth. This custom traces its origins to the Acts of the Apostles, in which we read that converts to the faith often entered the Church as a household, which might include husband, wife, children, and even their slaves.

Those who come into the Church as adults make their pilgrimage in what is called the RCIA, or Rite of Christian Initiation of Adults. Both for adults and for children, the sacraments of initiation are baptism, confirmation, and Eucharist.

BAPTISM: THE DOOR TO THE SACRAMENTS

They go down into the water dead.
Living they come up again.
The Son of God will rejoice among them
and be glad when he receives his people washed clean.
            —The Shepherd of Hermas, about AD 140–150

When a child is about to be baptized, the priest or deacon meets and greets the parents at the door of the church, and leads them to the place of baptism, the font or baptistery, which is usually close to the door of the church building. *The Catechism of the Catholic Church* refers to baptism, the first of the seven sacraments, as a door that gives access to the other sacraments (#1213). In this sacrament of initiation, we begin a new life in Christ and the Holy Spirit, are incorporated into the Church, and, for those not baptized as infants, forgiven of any sins we may have committed. Baptism enlightens us with the Spirit's grace that, together with all the Church, we might respond to the call of Christ which we hear in the gospel.

This first of the three sacraments of initiation (confirmation and Eucharist complete our initiation) frees us from the power of darkness called original sin. Going down into the water, we die and are buried with Christ. Rising up out of the water, we emerge as sons and daughters of God and, together with all the Church, are formed into God's people.

Later, signed with the gift of the Spirit in confirmation (the second sacrament of initiation), we more perfectly become the image of the Lord and commit ourselves even more eagerly to building up the Body of Christ. Finally, we come to the table of the Eucharist (the third sacrament of initiation), which reflects the unity of God's people nourished with the Body and Blood of Christ.

The Catechism of the Catholic Church (#1267) teaches that baptism incorporates us into the Church; we become members of the Body of Christ. Tertullian, a second-century writer, regarded as a father of the Church, commented that Christians are "made, not born."

In some Christian denominations children are not baptized until they are old enough to ask for baptism and to have some idea of what it means and why it is important. Catholics have always baptized infants and children. A child who cannot yet speak can hardly profess the Creed, the statement of those truths that binds the Church together. From the earliest of Christian times, however, as we read in the Acts of the Apostles, the Church has baptized children as well as adults. The parents select godparents who will model the practice of faith for the child. The parents and godparents, representing the local Church and all the saints and all believers everywhere, profess faith for the child who will later be formed in the faith into which he or she has been baptized.

CONFIRMATION: SEALED WITH THE GIFT OF THE HOLY SPIRIT

But you will receive power when the holy Spirit comes upon you, and you will be my witnesses in Jerusalem, throughout Judea and Samaria, and to the ends of the earth.

—Acts 1:8

A bishop and theologian from southern France in the mid-fifth century observed, in a Pentecost homily, that in baptism we are regenerated, coming to new life; after baptism, we are confirmed for the struggle. Confirmation strengthens one for the Christian life with the gifts of the Holy Spirit. These gifts are enumerated in the prayer said by the bishop as he lays hands on or extends hands over the candidates. He prays that those who have been given new life in baptism may now receive God's Spirit as helper and guide, giving us the gifts of wisdom and understanding, right judgment and courage, knowledge and reverence, and the spirit of wonder and awe in God's good presence. So confirmation completes the sacrament of baptism.

Those who enter the Church as adults receive the sacraments of initiation in their historical order: baptism, confirmation, Eucharist. Those born into Catholic families, however, most often receive the sacrament of confirmation after first communion. This practice may seem a bit confusing.

EUCHARIST: PARTICIPATION IN THE BODY OF CHRIST

Since this fountain, this source of life,
this table surrounds us with untold blessings
and fills us with the gifts of the Spirit,
let us approach it with sincerity of heart
and purity of conscience
to receive grace and mercy in our time of need.
                    —John Chrysostom, *The Catecheses*

The Apostle Paul's first letter to the Church at Corinth contains one of the oldest descriptions of the Christian Eucharist. It is brief, but powerful. He asks an energetic question that calls for a great "Amen!" from all the Church. "The cup of blessing that we bless, is it not a participation in the blood of Christ? The bread that we break, is it not a participation in the body of Christ? Because the loaf of bread is one, we, though many, are one body, for we all partake of the one loaf" (1 Cor 10:16–17).

Paul summarizes what Christians do around book and table: gathering, offering, blessing, breaking, pouring, eating, drinking, and sharing. In this activity, we are joined to the Christ who assembles us, and whose Spirit lives both within the individual Christian and, importantly, in the gathered community. Thus, we are joined in the eucharistic activity one to another in which we are fed with food and drink that the Church asserts has become the true and substantial presence of Christ. At the eucharistic table, Christians are incorporated into Christ. Our lives are touched by and embodied into the very life of God. Because we are the Body of Christ, we are united so intimately that loving service one of another is the logical consequence of what we have done and what we have become.

RECONCILIATION: PARDON AND PEACE

In the gospels, we encounter Jesus who "came to Galilee proclaiming the gospel of God: 'This is the time of fulfillment. The kingdom of God is at hand. Repent, and believe in the gospel'" (Mark 1:14–15). Thus we know that repentance is a constant in Christian life; this realization prompts the faithful Catholic to seek out the sacrament of reconciliation, sometimes called penance or confession.

The effects of the sacrament of reconciliation are wonderfully described in the celebration's prayer of absolution: "God the Father of mercies, / through the death and resurrection of his Son / has reconciled the world to himself / and sent the Holy Spirit among us / for the forgiveness of sins; / through the ministry of the Church / may God give you pardon and peace, / and I absolve you from your sins / in the name of the Father, and of the Son, / and of the Holy Spirit."

The Christian life is about *metanoia*, conversion of hearts and minds and attitudes. The sacrament of reconciliation offers the opportunity to reflect on our sinfulness, confess our sins, repent of our wickedness, accept a penance, and be reconciled with one's self, with the Church, and with God.

CONFESSION: A HOW-TO GUIDE FOR THE ANXIOUS OR RELUCTANT

We have come to know and to believe in the love God has for us. God is love, and whoever remains in love remains in God and God in him. In this is love brought

to perfection among us, that we have confidence on the
day of judgment because as he is, so are we in this world.
There is no fear in love, but perfect love drives out fear
because fear has to do with punishment, and so one who
fears is not yet perfect in love.

—1 John 4:16–18

Many Catholics have anxiety about approaching the sacrament of reconciliation. Some fear that the priest will announce to them and to all in earshot, "You deserve to be run over by a bus." There is no reliable report of such an outrage ever really happening. But when we bring such fears to the sacrament that is intended to bring pardon and peace, we might legitimately ask if we are not candidates for the sin of pride. Are our sins really so special, so terribly unique, that the priest will be reduced to openmouthed shock at hearing them? Unlikely.

The formula is simple. Entering the appointed spot, usually a confessional or reconciliation chapel (though the sacrament can be celebrated anywhere), the penitent makes the Sign of the Cross and says, "Bless me, Father, for I have sinned." Usually, she or he will say how long it has been since last confessing, and then mention the sins committed and how often each has occurred. The penitent concludes, saying, "I am sorry for these and all the sins of my past life."

The priest may comment, offer encouragement, suggest a penance, and invite the penitent to express sorrow and contrition (see the Act of Contrition in the prayer section near the end of this book). Finally, the priest, with hands extended over the penitent, says the prayer of absolution.

Some Catholics brought up to confess their sins frequently, will be heard to complain that they are weary "of confessing the same old sins over and over again." It should be understood that this is a condemnation neither of the Church nor of the sacrament, but is rather something of a personal indictment. The Christian hopes to grow not just in age, but in wisdom and grace as well. Those who lament loudly that their list of sins is unchanging and repetitive might be revealing a certain spiritual stagnation or inability to examine their consciences in a meaningful way that might lead to repentance and growth.

The focus of the sacrament is not guilt, but grace. And as those who have gone before us remind, grace will lead us on.

MARRIAGE: COVENANT OF LOVE

God created man in his image;
in the divine image he created him;
male and female he created them.
God blessed them, saying: "Be fertile and multiply; fill the
earth and subdue it. Have dominion over the fish of the
sea, the birds of the air, and all the living things that move
on the earth."

—Genesis 1:27–28

Marriage is the sacrament through which God creates the future of both the world and the Church. One of the prayers after communion from the wedding Mass gives a succinct description of what is going on in Christian marriage. Speaking to God in the midst of the Church, the priest prays to God who has made the bride and groom one in marriage and in the sharing of the one bread and the one cup. The Church asks that God make the couple one in their love for each other.

The bride and groom are themselves the ministers of the sacrament; the priest is the Church's witness. He asks them three questions about freedom, faithfulness, and children that are answered publicly by both. Those entering marriage assert that they come freely and without reservation, that they will love and honor each other as husband and wife until death, and that they will accept children lovingly from God, bringing them up according to the law of Christ and the Church.

The marriage relationship is clearly unique; in it, the human relationship becomes a mirror or sacrament of the love of God. This love goes beyond its ordinary meaning and brings new life to the world.

The marriage vows are noble in their simplicity and give a clear statement of what the husband and wife seek to do in cooperation with God's love: "I, N., take you, N., to be my wife/husband. I promise to be true to you in good times and in bad, in sickness and in health. I will love you and honor you all the days of my life."

HOLY ORDERS: SET APART FOR SERVICE

There are different kinds of spiritual gifts but the same Spirit; there are different forms of service but the same Lord; there are different workings but the same God who produces all of them in everyone. To each individual the manifestation of the Spirit is given for some benefit.

—1 Cor 12:4–7

The sacrament of holy orders is, as the name suggests, about bringing order to God's Church. It is not about personal honor or prestige, but instead assembles a college of ministers who have corporate responsibility for the life of the Church. The model for such leadership is found in an exhortation from the First Letter of Peter: "Tend the flock of God in your midst, (overseeing) not by constraint but willingly, as God would have it, not for shameful profit but eagerly. Do not lord it over those assigned to you, but be examples to the flock" (5:2–3).

Through the laying on of hands, the power of the Holy Spirit is given to bishops, priests, and deacons for the good of the Church. Gathered around a local bishop, who is a successor to the apostles, the priests and deacons share his ministry in proclaiming the word, directing the community, and ensuring mutual service.

Each of the baptized is called to service in the Church; the varied and cooperative ministries of the ordained and nonordained remind all that Christ is the head of the Church, and the apostolic ministry is a reminder in every age that it is Christ who sends and we who are sent. Those who are ordained as bishops, priests (sometimes also called presbyters), and deacons have the example of Jesus himself to follow: "I am among you as the one who serves" (Luke 22:27). They are charged to proclaim the word, preside at common worship, guide the community in discerning the call of the Holy Spirit, and to provide pastoral leadership.

On the day of ordination, speaking to the newly ordained, the bishop echoes St. Paul's Letter to the Philippians: "The one who began a good work in you will continue to complete it until the day of Christ Jesus" (1:6). The entire community prays day by day for this group of leaders and for all the Church. The third Eucharistic Prayer asks God to strengthen both in faith and love the Church in pilgrimage on earth, which includes the pope as bishop of Rome, our local bishops, with the clergy and the entire people gained for God by Christ.

ANOINTING OF THE SICK: CONFIDENCE IN DIVINE MERCY

In John's Gospel, we read the story of the man born blind. The fellow explains wonderfully what Jesus did: "One thing I do know is that I was blind and now I see" (9:25). Clearly, one of the points of the story is that we are all blind in one way or another, so John's telling of the tale is not just about physical healing. The story is also a meditation on baptism and the search for faith.

The healing Christ is not confined to gospel times but moves about in our midst today. Thus, the Church provides a ritual for those who are seriously ill. The inspiration comes from the healing activity of Jesus and from the Letter of James: "Is anyone among you sick? He should summon the presbyters of the church, and they should pray over him and anoint [him] with oil in the name of the Lord, and the prayer of faith will save the sick person, and the Lord will raise him up. If he has committed any sins, he will be forgiven" (5:14–15).

A priest lays hands on those to be anointed and then anoints their brows ("Through this holy anointing, / may the Lord in his love and mercy help you / with the grace of the Holy Spirit") and their hands ("May the Lord who frees you from sin / save you and raise you up"). Those who seek the sacrament do so with faith, which enables them to accept with valor, or faithful resignation, the infirmities that may lead in the end to death. The Council of Trent taught, and the Church teaches still, that the sacrament relieves and strengthens the sick person, arousing great confidence in God's divine mercy.

Those who seek the sacrament today understand their faith as the prayers of the Church present it. The first

Preface of Christian Death from the funeral Mass highlights the faith that prompts the elderly and infirm to seek the sacrament, believing that, though death is inevitable, sadness gives way to immortality's bright promise. Life is changed rather than ended. Further, the earthly body that lies in death will find a dwelling place in heaven.

Thus, we see the two possible graced results of the sacrament, as Trent taught and as the Church still teaches: Those who are anointed may be strengthened in their suffering. Sometimes, they may regain bodily health if God judges that course to be expedient for the health of the soul.

WHO CAN BRING COMMUNION TO THE SICK?

Bringing communion to the sick reminds them and us that they are full members of the community even when infirmity might make coming to the parish church for Mass impossible. In fact, the original purpose of reserving the Eucharist was to make it possible to bring communion to the sick or to offer *viaticum*, food for the journey, the last communion before death.

Many parishes depute faithful members to visit the sick, to pray with them, and to bring them the Eucharist. Usually, they read together the gospel appointed for the Mass of the day and pray the Lord's Prayer, after which they are given the parish bulletin and any news of the community.

WHAT'S RCIA?

The Rite of Christian Initiation of Adults, the RCIA, is about becoming one with the Church, about initiation and incorporation, and about *metanoia*, the transformation of our hearts and minds and attitudes. This transformation of lives is in cooperation with God's grace and the call of the Holy Spirit.

The liturgical celebrations by which one enters and is welcomed into the Church are not the whole of the life of the Church, but rather the source, summit, and climax of the journey, steps along the way to becoming one with Christ. Sacramental grace is not given just at the moment a sacrament is conferred, but it is the enduring gift and presence of God's transforming Spirit, always at work in the hearts and lives of believers.

Thus, the RCIA is a type of journey or pilgrimage; the process does not run as an academic year and will not proceed at the same pace for all people. As in most pilgrimages, some move forward with speedy decisiveness, others move in more slowly. There are three stages: becoming a catechumen, or a learner; participating in the rite of election or enrollment; and, finally, celebrating the three sacraments of initiation, which are baptism, Eucharist, and confirmation.

The catechumenate follows the ancient practice of the Church that was restored, revised, and adapted to contemporary needs and circumstances by the Second Vatican Council. The initiation of catechumens is the work both of the whole Church and of individual parishes; catechumens and the faithful together reflect on the paschal mystery. The faithful have the opportunity to renew their own conversion and, says the introduction to the rite, "by their example lead the catechumens to obey the Holy Spirit more generously" (1:4). Thus does the Spirit of God renew the Church in every age.

THE FUNERAL RITE: SURE AND CERTAIN HOPE

O God,
in whom sinners find mercy and the saints find joy,
we pray to you for our brother [sister] N.,
whose body we honor with Christian burial,
that he [she] may be delivered from the bonds of death.
Admit him [her] to the joyful company of your saints
and raise him [her] on the last day
to rejoice in your presence forever.
We ask this through our Lord Jesus Christ, your Son,
who lives and reigns with you and the Holy Spirit,
one God for ever and ever.
Amen.

—Funeral Mass, Opening Prayer C

At a Catholic funeral, we do not want to depend on human eloquence or on our understanding of providence and grace to make sense of our loss and sorrow. The Church's ritual and prayer affirm why we live, and our common belief in the Communion of Saints gives us hope. The Rite of Funerals, revised by decree of the Second Vatican Council, notes that the Church's funeral custom has been, not only to commend the dead to God, but also to support the Christian hope of the people and to give witness to their faith in the future resurrection of the baptized with Christ.

St. Augustine reminds us in his essay "On the Care for the Dead" that funeral arrangements, the grave, and the ceremonies are more a solace for survivors than aid for the dead. The Church intercedes for the dead in confident belief that death is not the end and does not break the bonds forged in life.

A community gathers around the body of a loved one, performing rituals, repeating certain words, singing psalms, hymns, and inspired songs, and calling upon God to affirm that love is stronger than death. Good ritual makes all of this clear. The reception and opening of the casket; the closing of the casket in farewell; the music and prayers; the symbols of light, water, and the white pall; the Scripture selections; the homily; communion, the core action of the eucharistic liturgy; and the final commendation—all of this conveys powerfully the Gospel of Life with all its implications for how the living go forth from the church and the cemetery, and back into their lives.

One who listens carefully to the funeral prayers will go away with an enriched understanding of how Christians view death. The ritual includes receiving the body at the door of the church, readings from Scripture, and the celebration of the Eucharist. The liturgy ends not at the altar but at the grave. Attentive to what we believe, pray, and celebrate, we can walk from the grave "in the sure and certain hope that, together with all who have died in Christ," the faithful will rise on the last day.

IV

BUT, THEN, WHAT ABOUT...?

Christian, remember your dignity,
and now that you share in God's own nature,
do not return by sin to your former base condition.
Bear in mind who is your head
and of whose body you are a member.
Do not forget that you have been rescued
from the power of darkness
and brought into the light of God's kingdom.

—Leo the Great
from a fifth-century nativity homily

CAN I SOLVE THE PASCHAL MYSTERY?

This is a mystery not to be solved but to be lived. The second Memorial Acclamation at the Eucharist succinctly states the content of the paschal mystery: "Dying you destroyed our death, / rising you restored our life. / Lord Jesus, come in glory." This mystery is present in the Church, most especially when the Church is gathered at the eucharistic table.

The term *paschal* comes from the Jewish feast of Passover, which commemorates the deliverance of the Jews from slavery by the blood of the sacrificed lamb sprinkled on their doorposts so that the angel of death would "pass over" and spare their homes and their firstborn. Jesus is the new Lamb of God by whose blood we are saved.

WHY DO WE NO LONGER SAY *YAHWEH*?

The Vatican's Congregation for Divine Worship and the Discipline of the Sacraments directed in 2008 that the word *Lord* be used instead of *Yahweh* in English-language worship, just as the Hebrews and early Christians substituted other names for *Yahweh* when reading Scripture aloud. The word is considered the sacred name of God and is derived from the ancient Hebrew rendering, which used only the consonants YHWH.

The directive, which seeks to be sensitive both to biblical tradition and to Christianity's Jewish heritage, requires the revision of some popular songs, including "You Are Near," a version of Psalm 139 that begins "Yahweh, I know you are near."

After the publication of the *Jerusalem Bible*—a translation with the Vatican's imprimatur that consistently uses the word *Yahweh*—the term was used more frequently in English. The name is known as the "divine tetragrammaton," and speaking it aloud is considered offensive by many Jews.

WHEN DOES LENT END?

Catholics of a certain age often wondered (and heard various answers) about when Lent ended. Lent ends as we begin the Easter Triduum, celebrating the Mass of the Lord's Supper on Holy Thursday. The rubrics, or guides for our ritual celebrations, settle it by instructing us in the Sacramentary that on Holy Thursday the Easter celebration has begun:

"During the singing of the Gloria, the church bells are rung and then remain silent until the Easter Vigil, unless the conference of bishops or the Ordinary decrees otherwise." We still fast on Good Friday and until the Easter Vigil begins, but it is not the Lenten fast of penance and preparation: it is anticipatory fast. The *Constitution on the Sacred Liturgy* (#110) alerts us to this important distinction. The Lenten penance is internal and individual, but at the same time external and social. The practice of Lenten penance should be fostered according to the circumstances of the faithful in different places and times and encouraged by those who are in authority. The paschal fast, on Good Friday and, when possible, prolonged through Holy Saturday, is to be kept sacred so that we come to Sunday's Easter joy with clear, uplifted minds.

WHERE DID WE GET THE NAME *EASTER*?

Our English name *Easter* was taken from the name of Eostre, the Anglo-Saxon goddess of the rising light of day and spring. The greatest feast of the Church year celebrates the resurrection of Christ, God's triumph over sin and death. Because Christ is the Light of the World and because light conquers darkness, it seemed both perfectly logical and symbolic to claim the ancient name of the goddess for the feast and to celebrate it close to the vernal equinox when, at least in the northern hemisphere, winter gives way to spring and new life.

WHAT'S A TRIDUUM?
WHAT'S AN OCTAVE?

The Easter celebration is called the Triduum, or the Great Three Days. The rites of the Triduum explain what we believe about the passion, death, and resurrection of Jesus and about our own place in that paschal mystery. The celebration begins with the Thursday evening Mass of the Lord's Supper, continues with the Good Friday Commemoration of the Lord's Passion, and the Great Vigil of Easter. The Holy Thursday service takes place after sundown, so the three days are actually Friday, Saturday, and Sunday, following Jewish tradition, which regards a day as beginning after sundown on the previous evening.

Today, the Church continues only the Christmas and Easter celebrations for an octave, eight days, a period of prolonged rejoicing because the God of all creation has entered into human time and space with the promise of eternal life. The Church prays with the psalmist: "This is the day the Lord has made; let us rejoice in it and be glad" (Ps 118:24).

WHY IS EASTER A MOVEABLE FEAST?

The Easter celebration shifts—moves—every year. Easter is celebrated on the first Sunday after the first full moon following the vernal equinox, March 21. Easter then can be as early as March 22 or as late as April 25. Because the date changes from year to year, it is called a moveable feast.

IS THE IDEA OF SIN OR SINFULNESS OUT OF FASHION?

No. Neither sin nor sinfulness has ceased to exist, even if the terms or concepts seem somehow out of step in contemporary society. The human condition, original sin, or the power of darkness all describe our tendency to make poor or selfish choices that sometimes harm others, the community, and ourselves. This activity, depending on our intentions, could be sinful.

GRACE: THE GIFT THAT KEEPS ON GIVING

In the beginning was the Word, and the Word was with God, and the Word was God.

He was in the beginning with God. All things came to be through him, and without him nothing came to be. What came to be through him was life, and this life was the light of the human race; the light shines in the darkness, and the darkness has not overcome it....

And the Word became flesh and made his dwelling among us, and we saw his glory, the glory as of the Father's only Son, full of grace and truth.

—John 1:1–5, 14

Grace is participation in the life of God (*Catechism* #1997). Grace is free and undeserved; it helps us respond to God's call to fullness of life (#1996). God's initiative invites human response.

The Word at work among us allows us glimpses of God's glory, the foretaste and promise of that which awaits us. Art and popular culture at their very best celebrate this glory: grace and truth at work. For example, George Bernanos enfleshes John's gospel-vision in his fictional autobiography of a soul, *Diary of a Country Priest*, a literary imitation of St. Augustine's *Confessions* or St. Thérèse of Lisieux's *Story of a Soul*.

The youthful, frail country priest is advised by a neighboring pastor: "Keep order all day long, knowing full well disorder will win out tomorrow." But the younger cleric has a more inspired, hopeful vision; he asserts that "Grace is everywhere." He knows, as we who stand under the gospel must also know, that because the Word became flesh and dwells among us, we will see here and hereafter the glory of God, full of grace and truth.

WHY IS IT CALLED THE *MASS*?

When the liturgy is celebrated in Latin, the dismissal is *Ite, Missa est*. This literally means, "Go, it is sent." The congregation responds, *Deo gratias*, "Thanks be to God." They are not giving thanks that the Mass is ended, but rather are responding to the dismissal, which would be more correctly understood as a commissioning. The congregation, having celebrated the mysteries that give life, is sent forth to bring what they have experienced to all the world. The congregants are sent forth to share the apostolic task. The term *Missa* came to mean the whole Rite of the Eucharist and gives us the English term *Mass*.

WHAT IS THE LITURGY OF THE HOURS?

The Church's official daily prayer recited at particular times of the day is the Liturgy of the Hours traditionally known as the Divine Office and sometimes called the "Breviary" (after the prayer book that contains all the necessary texts). It consists of the psalms (which are often called the Church's prayer book) with hymns and Scripture readings. While monks, nuns, priests, and deacons are obliged to pray the Hours daily, the prayer belongs to the entire Church and many laypeople join in praying the Hours, either privately or in groups. Many books and Internet resources facilitate praying the Hours.

There are seven traditional hours of prayer: Matins or Vigils, often said at night in monasteries, Lauds in the early morning, Terce at midmorning, Sext at midday, Nones at midafternoon, Vespers in the evening, and Compline at night.

WHERE DID THE "EIGHTH DAY" COME FROM?

In the first creation story, Genesis details God's work in fashioning the earth and reports that "God blessed the seventh day and made it holy, because on it he rested from all the work he had done in creation" (2:3).

Saturday is the seventh day of the week, the day marked as the Sabbath. Because the resurrection took place on Sunday, the first day of the week, Christians eventually transferred the Sabbath rest to Sunday. It is sometimes called the "eighth day" because it signifies a new creation and a new life. The author of the Book of Revelation reports seeing a new heaven and a new earth, and he heard a loud voice: "And the One who sat upon the throne said, 'Behold, I make all things new'" (21:5).

Sometimes baptismal fonts or even churches are constructed with eight sides; this feature recalls that in Christ, all of creation is renewed.

WAS JESUS REALLY BORN ON DECEMBER 25?

Neither Scripture nor Tradition tells us the day or even the season when Jesus was born. But all cultures have celebrated the solstice in joyful hope, when the earth has turned so that daylight no longer diminishes but increases day by day. Because Christ is the Light of the World, what better time to celebrate light's triumph over darkness than when the season itself suggests the holy truth?

WHAT'S UP WITH CHRISTMAS TREES? ARE THEY REALLY PAGAN SYMBOLS?

Some suggest that Christmas trees are to be discouraged because they are pagan symbols. Perhaps they were pagan symbols of something or other thousands of years ago. But, really, does anyone at all ever see an evergreen in a church or home today and think that the people who put it up are, in fact, suggesting something non-Christian? Over the course of the years, the evergreen has become a symbol of the One born among us who, by rising from the dead, conquered sin and death. Festivity and delight and even the decoration of homes follow such a belief, even before theology can reflect on the wondrous teaching. Those who see a tinseled tree as a threat to all this have lost sight of the forest.

WHAT'S THE DIFFERENCE BETWEEN ECUMENICAL AND INTERFAITH?

Jesus prayed "that they all may be one" (John 17:21), and in those words the splintered Christian Church finds the inspiration and the reason to continue dialogue with the vision of restoring the unity of God's Church. Ecumenical relationships are those among Christians and Christian denominations who are seeking to discover, not just the differences between us, but our shared strengths and concerns.

Interfaith relationships are those among Christians and other faith traditions in which Jesus is not regarded as Lord, including but not limited to Judaism, Islam, Buddhism, and Hinduism. It is important for Catholic people to remember that the Second Vatican Council (1962–65) taught that the Church does not reject anything holy or true in other religions, that the Church has a high regard for their way of life, and that, even though we differ on many points, we often see in the world's religions reflected rays of truth (*Nostra Aetate* 2).

Cooperative, respectful, and positive interaction is sure to lead not just to tolerance but to true peace.

V

QUESTIONS FROM THE TRADITION

What are humans that you are mindful of them,
mere mortals that you care for them?
Yet you have made them little less than a god,
crowned them with glory and honor.

—Psalm 8:5–6

WHO ARE THE FATHERS OF THE CHURCH?

The fathers of the Church are writers, theologians, laymen, deacons, and bishops from the earliest Christian centuries who articulated and shaped Church teaching. These predecessors in the faith helped shaped the Church in its infancy and first centuries. Usually, the term *early Church* includes the apostolic times until the Council of Ephesus in 431.

WHO ARE THE DOCTORS OF THE CHURCH?

The term *doctor* comes from the Latin *docere*, which means to teach. Certain writers whose teachings have illuminated the Church are awarded that title. From the period of the Church fathers, Ss. Gregory the Great, Ambrose, Augustine, and Jerome in the West are given that honor; in the East, Ss. John Chrysostom, Basil, Athanasius, and Gregory Nazianzen are venerated. At the moment, there are thirty-three doctors, including three women: Ss. Teresa of Avila, Catherine of Siena, and Thérèse of Lisieux.

The criteria for being named a doctor of the Church are eminence in learning, high holiness, and proclamation by the Church through a declaration by the pope or a council.

WHAT ARE THE SEVEN DEADLY SINS AND THE SEVEN CONTRARY VIRTUES?

The seven deadly sins are vices that are threats to salvation and that diminish both persons and the human community. They include lust, gluttony, greed, sloth, wrath, envy, and pride. The seven virtues—called "contrary" because they oppose and are the opposites of these vices— were first enumerated in the poem *Psychomachia*, "Contest of the Soul," by the Spanish poet Aurelius Clemens Prudentius about AD 410; the poem details the battle of good and evil. Practicing the virtues counteracts the temptations of the seven deadly sins. The virtues are chastity, temperance, charity, diligence, patience, kindness, and humility. They are the result of living responsively to the gifts of the Holy Spirit given in confirmation.

IS MARY A GODDESS?

No, Mary is not a goddess. But as the Mother of Jesus, Mary is also regarded as the Mother of God. The First Council of Nicaea in 325 affirmed that Jesus is God, consubstantial, or one in being with, the Father. The Council of Ephesus in 431 taught that Mary is the Mother of Jesus who is God Incarnate. Since then, she has been referred to as *Theotokos*, or God-bearer.

In the Magnificat, Mary's song of praise in Luke's Gospel, she gives thanks to God: "The Mighty One has done great things for me, and holy is his name" (1:49). The alternative opening prayer for Mass on the feast of the annunciation (March 25) highlights Mary's mission when the Church asks God that her prayers bring Jesus to the waiting world, filling the void of incompletion with her child's presence.

St. Amadeus of Lausanne (a Cistercian monk who in 1144 became a bishop in what is now France) wrote of Mary as a gentle and affectionate bride, the mother of the true bridegroom. In goodness, she channels the life-giving waters of reason that surround the shores of all nations. With God's assistance, she redirects pools of grace.

WHAT ARE THE SEVEN SORROWS OF MARY?

The Seven Sorrow, or Dolors, of Mary, are all found in the gospels. They include the prophecy of Simeon, the flight into Egypt, the loss of the child Jesus in the Temple, meeting Jesus on the way to Calvary, the crucifixion, the removal of his body from the cross, and placing his body in the tomb.

The memorial day of Our Lady of Sorrows is on September 15, the day after the feast of the Triumph, sometimes called the Exaltation, of the Holy Cross. This proximity of feasts puts Mary's sorrows into the proper context: that of the saving death and resurrection of Jesus.

WHAT ABOUT CHURCHES THAT SOUND EASTERN ORTHODOX BUT ARE IN COMMUNION WITH THE POPE?

Eastern Orthodox Churches that are not in full communion with Rome are nonetheless in deep communion with the Catholic Church and celebrate true sacraments. Within the Catholic Church, there are a number of rites or diverse liturgical traditions. These include the Roman and Ambrosian Rites, the Byzantine, Coptic, Syriac, Armenian, Maronite, and Chaldean Rites. Over all of these, the pope reigns as pontiff, meaning bridge builder, and Servant of the Servants of God.

WHY DO WE BURN CANDLES WHEN WE PRAY?

Christ is the Light of the World. Any lighted candle reminds Christians of this truth. In ancient times, and today when electrical power fades, candles also allow folks to see; in that capacity, too, they serve as a sacramental, illumining all the world with the light of Christ.

WHAT IS THE DIFFERENCE BETWEEN A CATHEDRAL AND A BASILICA?

A cathedral is the bishop's church in which is found his *cathedra*, or chair, which is symbolic of his role as chief teacher in his diocese. A basilica is a church building that has been given special status and privilege, often because of its history. A unique feature of the basilica is an umbrella or canopy of red and yellow silk, the colors of the papal government, topped by a copper cross. The original function of the umbrella was to shelter the patriarch; now, its function is to signify that the building has been designated a basilica since at least some of these buildings do not adhere to the original form of Roman architecture.

Four major basilicas are found in Rome: St. John Lateran, which is the pope's cathedral; St. Peter's in Vatican City; St. Paul's Outside the Walls; and St. Mary Major.

HOW IS THE POPE ELECTED?

After the death and burial of a pope, the cardinals of the Church who are under eighty years of age meet in the Sistine Chapel in a conclave (a word that comes from the Latin for "with a key," from an era in which they were actually locked in). By a secret vote with paper ballots, they elect the next pope.

WHY DO WE SAY "LAMB OF GOD"?

Lamb of God is a title given to Christ in the New Testament. It makes reference to the saving activity of his death and resurrection. The Old Testament Book of Exodus (12:1–28) relates the story of the ancient Passover in which the Israelites were spared after slaughtering a lamb and marking their doors with its blood. Jesus is the new Lamb who lives forever and by whose outpoured blood we are saved.

WHY DO WE SOMETIMES SAY "TWO TABLES" WHEN SPEAKING OF THE EUCHARIST?

Fifteenth-century monk Thomas à Kempis wrote in his book *The Imitation of Christ* that two things were necessary to make life tolerable: food and light. He observes that God has given to us who are weak the Body and Blood of Christ to refresh us, and has set before us the Word as a lantern for our feet. He calls these gifts two tables. Thus the two tables are of Word and Eucharist: the Liturgy of the Word and the Liturgy of the Eucharist, together the two parts of the Mass.

VI

CONTEMPORARY CHALLENGES

The quality of holiness is shown
Not by what we say but by what we do in life.
> —St. Gregory of Nyssa
> from a treatise on *Christian Perfection*

CATHOLIC MANNERS

No foul language should come out of your mouths, but only such as is good for needed edification, that it may impart grace to those who hear. And do not grieve the holy Spirit of God, with which you were sealed for the day of redemption. All bitterness, fury, anger, shouting, and reviling must be removed from you, along with all malice. [And] be kind to one another, compassionate, forgiving one another as God has forgiven you in Christ.

So be imitators of God, as beloved children, and live in love, as Christ loved us and handed himself over for us as a sacrificial offering to God for a fragrant aroma.
> —Eph 4:29—5:2

This is a challenging age in which many seem to confuse their own opinions with revealed truth. Surely this is a dangerous stance. While Catholics give assent to the status of the Church as both Mother and Teacher, this does not mean that we give up our own freedom and conscience. In fact, the Church's law stipulates that we are bound to seek the truth and have the right to embrace and observe the truth that we have come to know (Can #748 §1). This canon seems to highlight the priority of conscience celebrated in Vatican II's *Constitution on the Church in the Modern World* (*Gaudium et spes*), which tells us a number of things about conscience. First, conscience speaks to our hearts and helps us detect a law that is not of our making, but one which we must obey. The conscience summons us to do good and avoid evil. In the conscience, our most secret core and sanctuary, we are alone with God. The divine voice echoes there, revealing the law of God, which is fulfilled when we love God and one another (#16).

Following one's conscience is not, however, an excuse to be less than civil. In a Church that includes some zany members, as well as folks who are sometimes hurtful in their pursuit of the gospel call that they hear, remembering one's manners is a very high call. Even small matters of incivility must be avoided by those who will to build the enduring and coming reign of God. Those who see themselves as orthodox protectors of a disappearing or diminishing tradition, even in their alarm, really ought not to consider themselves free of the same obligation to behave in a mannerly fashion. Neither are those annoyed with the orthodox protectors free from the call to manners. Both approaches are cankers on the Body of Christ.

Differences may certainly be aired as God's people seek ways to live together better, building up God's reign. But each must take seriously the challenge heard in Ephesians: "So then, putting away falsehood, let all of us speak the truth to our neighbors, for we are members of one another. Be angry but do not sin; do not let the sun go down on your anger, and do not make room for the devil" (Eph 4:25–27).

THE CHALLENGE: TELEVISION AND POPULAR CULTURE

Prime-time situation comedies are not pornographic, do not present a threat to national security, and probably will not cause cancer in laboratory animals. But whether they reflect the nation's values or shape those values is the beginning of a significant discussion. Popular culture might reflect the sensibilities and tensions of an age even while offending the sensitivities of the religious minority whose responsibilities ought to include working seriously to understand religion's role in but not of the world and culture.

It does not take a social scientist to see that television clearly reaches and teaches. If it can inspire brand loyalty at outrageous prices and counteract other voices (the surgeon general's, for example), the issue seems to be not how it teaches character and values to children and teenagers, but what kind of character and which values are being so masterfully inculcated.

This early interpretation of the notion of being in but not of the world reflects John's Gospel, in which Jesus speaks to those who follow: "It was not you who chose me, but I who chose you and appointed you to go and bear fruit that will remain, so that whatever you ask the Father in my name he may give you. This I command you: love one another. If the world hates you, realize that it hated me first. If you belonged to the world, the world would love its own; but because you do not belong to the world, and I have chosen you out of the world, the world hates you" (John 15:16–19).

Today's Christians have as great a challenge as did the first followers to encounter the difficulty when the rubber of the Gospel hits the road of popular culture. A young child, present at a dinner where prime-time television was being discussed, said recently, "In our home, we don't watch that show." Here was a child quite secure as a member of the counterculture, one who does not do everything or buy everything or watch everything that we are led to believe everyone else is doing, watching, and buying.

This is not to suggest that modern culture is somehow bad or is threatening in all its forms to the Christian and the Christian community. Rather, the Christian and the Christian community are called not to accept wholesale those suggestions that stand in opposition to the way we have chosen to live, to the way that we are called to live by the gospel. Remember: the same switch used to power your television can also switch it off.

The child who said "In our home, we don't watch that show" discusses with her parents how visions of reality she encounters daily do not square with the gospel-centered life her family wished to live. Such actions and such discussions might serve as models of resistance for right-thinking, right-living, right-practicing Christians of a very orthodox persuasion.

HOW ARE WOMEN PART OF THE BIG PICTURE?

Vatican II seems to have answered this question with a challenge that has not yet been met. *Gaudium et spes* notes that women are involved in most every sphere of life and ought to be permitted to play their part fully. The Council notes that everyone has a duty to see that the specific and necessary participation of women in cultural life is both acknowledged and fostered (#60).

DO CATHOLICS HAVE ENVIRONMENTAL CONCERNS?

Yes, Catholics share the concerns of all who love the earth. For us, it is a religious issue as well as an environmental concern. In his 1979 encyclical *The Redeemer of Humanity*, Pope John Paul II addressed environmental issues. He wrote with certainty that it is God's will for humans to communicate with nature as intelligent masters and guardians, not as exploiters or destroyers.

Further in his 1987 encyclical *On Social Concern*, he claimed that dominion over creation is neither absolute power nor freedom to use and misuse as one pleases. Instead, there are moral issues to consider. Since from the very beginning of time, God has put limits on our use of the earth, as we see expressed symbolically in the story of the tree whose fruit was not to be eaten (Gen 2:16–17). John Paul II also addressed ecological concern, which he described as a greater realization of the limits of resources, and a greater realization of our need to respect nature and its cycles. Humanity's use and abuse of air, water, and soil that sustain all life is clearly a moral question.

IS IT A SIN TO NOT RECYCLE?

In 1991, the bishops of the United States outlined their understanding of the relationship between religious faith and reverence for the earth in a pastoral letter entitled "Renewing the Earth: An Invitation to Reflection and Action on Environment in Light of Catholic Social Teaching." The bishops assert that in Genesis, "God looked at everything he had made, and he found it very good" (Gen 1:31). Human beings, who are made in the image of God, share a unique responsibility to safeguard the created world and are called to enhance the world through their creative efforts.

The bishops see reverence for the earth based on the sacramental life of the Church, which uses created goods— water, oil, bread, and wine—to celebrate the transforming presence of Christ among us. We are left to ask how we can even consider spoiling or ruining water, soil, grapes, and wheat—fruits of the earth that are necessary to celebrate the sacraments.

So, is it a sin to pollute or to not recycle? Families and other groups are clearly called to consider the question.

HOW ABOUT THE SAINTS AND POPULAR DEVOTIONS?

The Preface to the Eucharistic Prayer for Masses of All Saints says succinctly what the Church believes and practices about the saints. God is glorified in the saints. In their lives, we are given an example. In our communion with them, we share God's friendship. In their prayer for the Church, we find strength and protection. As a great company of witnesses, they spur us on to glory that we might share their prize of everlasting glory in Christ.

Devotional practices play an important part in our spiritual life. What Pope Pius XII pointed out in 1947 remains true today: Devotional practices attract and direct our souls to God, purify us of sin, encourage us in virtue, and stimulate us in the path of sincere piety by teaching us to meditate on eternal truths and to better contemplate the human and divine natures of Christ (*Mediator Dei* 175).

IF THERE IS SEPARATION OF CHURCH AND STATE, SHOULD CATHOLICS VOTE?

Catholics are called to live lives of justice and peace. The United States Conference of Catholic Bishops asks Catholics to develop well-formed consciences to address political and social questions. Like all other citizens, they should bring these well-formed consciences into the voting booth.

IS ALL THEOLOGY ABOUT LIBERATION AND FREEDOM?

St. Anselm of Canterbury, in the eleventh century, described theology as "faith seeking understanding." People seek to illumine what they believe with reason and imagination. Much of theology invites Christians to critical reflection on action as a way of understanding God's disclosure, or revelation, of truth. Such action often includes work for justice and the dignity of all people as children of God, seeking both to understand and to alleviate human suffering. God's word is about justice and liberation. In this sense, we can regard theology as being about both liberation and freedom, because theology concerns our liberation from sin and death, as our eucharistic prayers remind us. The good news of the gospel is that death, suffering, and oppression will never have the final word.

DOES THE CHURCH HAVE ANYTHING TO SAY ABOUT SEX?

Vatican II's *Gaudium et spes* (1965) and Pope Paul VI's encyclical *Humanae vitae* (1968) rank love and procreation equally as the purposes of marriage. This shift in Church teaching raises love to the level of procreation, which, some suggest, shows an emerging awareness of women's equality. Because official Church teaching insists that every act of genital sexual activity must be part of a permanently committed, heterosexual love relationship, some claim that the Church has lost touch with current reality. Those who make such claims may not have explored Church teaching that sees God at work in our human activity, revealing the plan of divine love.

The *Declaration on Certain Questions Concerning Sexual Ethics* of 1975 observed that people in our time appear determined to discover, by the light of their own intelligence, the values innate in human nature in order to achieve an ever-greater development. He warns, though, that in moral matters, we cannot make value judgments according to personal whim, for in the depths of conscience, we detect a law that we do not impose on ourselves, but that calls us to obedience. This law in our hearts is written by God. To obey it is to find and celebrate our very dignity. We will be judged according to how well we have heard and obeyed that call to understand, promote, and live in and by that sublime dignity that is ours (3).

Catholics should take seriously this invitation to consider human sexuality and human conscience as gifts of the highest order.

IS THERE EITHER HEALING OR HOPE IN THE WAKE OF THE CLERGY SEXUAL ABUSE SCANDAL?

Writing in *Redemptoris Missio*, John Paul II noted that, because culture is a human creation and is therefore marked by sin, it too needs to be healed, ennobled, and perfected. The clergy sexual abuse scandal certainly offers proof both of the effects of original sin and of John Paul II's contention.

Australia's Bishop Geoffrey Robinson begins his book *Confronting Power and Sex in the Catholic Church: Reclaiming the Spirit of Jesus* by writing:

> Sexual abuse of minors by a significant number of priests and religious, together with attempts by many church authorities to conceal the abuse, constitute one of the ugliest stories ever to emerge from the Catholic Church. It is hard to imagine a more total contradiction of everything Jesus stood for, and it would be difficult to overestimate the pervasive and lasting harm it has done to the Church. (2008, p. 7)

Writing in *Clericalism: The Death of Priesthood*, Jesuit Fr. George B. Wilson judges that "the bishops' failure to recognize abuse by priests as a crime may or may not make them guilty in the eyes of the law; the feeble response they made to what they saw as a sin would earn them a failing grade in any respectable program for training of spiritual directors." He quotes Pope John Paul II's hope that the present crisis "must lead to a holier priesthood, a holier episcopate and a holier church" (2008, p. 74).

While any consideration of the crisis suggests that there is plenty of blame to go around, and that the consequences of both the abuse and the ineffectual response to it will be felt for a long time to come, Christians who believe in redemption and resurrection are called to seek out the grace that will enable true transformation of individuals, cultures, Church, and larger society.

WHAT DO CATHOLICS THINK ABOUT HOMOSEXUALITY AND MARRIAGE?

Catholic theology sees marriage as a unique relationship in that it nurtures and nourishes the husband and wife, while honoring the possibility that their love may issue forth in new life in cooperation with God's command in the Book of Genesis to increase and multiply.

There are other relationships among God's people. Some of these relationships are familial, social, or legal. Many of them are life-giving or affirming. Some may be either deleterious or sinful. No other relationships will obscure or change the Christian belief that God chooses to work through Christian marriage in populating both world and Church.

HOW ABOUT WAR, PEACE, AND ISSUES OF JUSTICE?

Catholics of all stripes and persuasions must be able to pray together as we search, wait, and work for peace. The tenor of the prayers in the Sacramentary balances theological and pastoral approaches following the example of the Perfect Example: Jesus, who touched the heart and healed the servant of the Roman centurion; Jesus, who raged against the hypocritical temple priests seeking to serve both civic pride and religious piety; Jesus, who wept over the city that did not recognize the hour of God's visitation—Jesus, the comforter, the pioneer and perfecter of our faith; Jesus, the merciful who will lead us and guide us through difficult dilemmas and dangerous days.

As Christians, we always pray for our enemies, that the Holy Spirit touch their hearts and turn their actions from terror to peace. We always pray that we never participate in intolerance or prejudice of any kind. We remember that the Church does not bless armies or policy goals or national interests, but rather blesses and prays for people.

IS THERE A CONSISTENT ETHIC OF LIFE? HOW DO WE LIVE IT?

Pope John Paul II may have answered this question in writing *Evangelica testificatio* ("On the renewal of the religious life according to the teaching of the Second Vatican Council"). He notes that from the very beginning, the Church's tradition and history show us a constant seeking for God, an undivided love for Christ, and a dedication to the growth of the kingdom. Without this activity, the charity that animates the Church could grow cold and the gospel be blunted. If this were to happen, the salt of faith would lose its savor.

He observes that the Holy Spirit stirs us up, putting us side by side with the martyrs and all the saints in every time and place. The life to which the Spirit calls us has the same value and vigor in every age. The Church could not live without these exceptional witnesses to the transcendence of the love of Christ that we see in every culture, in every land, and in every age. Imagine the sorry state of the world if these lights were to go out. So, the consistent ethic of life is seen in the variety and multiplicity of lives and lights that announce the kingdom of God with a liberty unfettered by obstacles and lived daily by thousands of daughters and sons of the Church (3).

VII

PRAYER

All of us, gazing with unveiled face on the glory of the Lord, are being transformed into the same image from glory to glory, as from the Lord who is the Spirit.
—2 Corinthians 3:18

TRADITIONAL CATHOLIC PRAYERS

The Lord's Prayer

Our Father
who art in heaven,
hallowed be thy name.
Thy kingdom come.
Thy will be done
on earth as it is in heaven.
Give us this day our daily bread,
and forgive us our trespasses
as we forgive those who trespass against us;
and lead us not into temptation
but deliver us from evil.
Amen.

The Hail Mary

Hail Mary, full of grace,
the Lord is with thee.
Blessed art thou among women
and blessed is the fruit of thy womb, Jesus.

Holy Mary, Mother of God,
pray for us sinners, now
and at the hour of our death.
Amen.

The Glory Be (Also known as the Doxology)

Glory be to the Father
and to the Son
and to the Holy Spirit.
As it was in the beginning,
is now, and ever shall be,
world without end.
Amen.

A Table Blessing

The eyes of all look hopefully to you;
you give them their food in due season.
You open wide your hand
and satisfy the desire of every living thing.
—Psalm 145:15–16

Traditional Prayer before Meals

Bless us, O Lord, and these thy gifts
which we are about to receive from thy bounty.
Through Christ our Lord. Amen.

Traditional Prayer after Meals

We give thee thanks, O Almighty God,
for these and all thy benefits.
And may the souls of the faithful departed,
through the mercy of God, rest in peace.
Amen.

A Sung Grace

John Wesley, the famous Methodist composer of hymns, wrote the following grace, which is usually sung to the tune for "Old One Hundreth."

Be present at our table, Lord;
Be here and everywhere adored.
Thy creatures bless and grant that we
May feast in paradise with thee.

An Act of Contrition

O my God, I am heartily sorry
for having offended thee,
and I detest all my sins
because of thy just punishments,

but most of all because they offend thee, my God,
Who are all-good and deserving of all my love.
I firmly resolve, with the help of thy grace,
to sin no more,
and to avoid the near occasions of sin.
Amen.

The Apostles' Creed

I believe in God, the Father Almighty,
creator of heaven and earth,
and in Jesus Christ,
his only Son, Our Lord,
who was conceived of the Holy Spirit,
born of the Virgin Mary,
suffered under Pontius Pilate,
was crucified, died, and was buried.
He descended to the dead.
On the third day he arose again.
He ascended into heaven,
and is seated at the right hand of the Father.
He will come again to judge the living and the dead.
I believe in the Holy Spirit,
the holy catholic Church,
the communion of saints,
the forgiveness of sins,
the resurrection of the body,
and life everlasting.
Amen.

Anima Christi

Soul of Christ, sanctify me.
Body of Christ, save me.
Blood of Christ, inebriate me.
Water from the side of Christ, wash me.
Passion of Christ, strengthen me.
O good Jesus, hear me.
Within thy wounds hide me.
Suffer me not to be separated from thee.
From the malignant enemy defend me.
In the hour of my death call me.
And bid me come unto thee,
That with thy saints I may praise thee
Forever and ever.
Amen.

The Guardian Angel Prayer

Angel of God, my guardian dear,
To whom God's love commits me here,
Ever this day [night] be at my side
To light and guard, to rule and guide.
Amen.

MARIAN PRAYERS

The Rosary

Around the first millennium, when literacy was uncommon, faithful Catholics often said the Rosary in place of the Liturgy of the Hours, the Church's official daily prayer composed of psalms, canticles, and Scripture readings. The practice developed gradually as ordinary people, who no longer learned the psalms, could substitute familiar prayers for them, such as the Lord's Prayer and the Hail Mary. Still a popular devotion today, the Rosary offers an opportunity to be quiet in God's good presence and to reflect on the mysteries that give life and hope in every age. Beads for the prayer are widely available. The odd practice of considering rosary beads a piece of jewelry, a necklace, or an ornament to hang from the rear-view mirror in one's car should be avoided, though carrying a rosary in one's pocket or purse as a reminder of Paul's injunction to "pray always" (1 Thess 5:17) is salutary.

The Rosary begins with the Apostles' Creed, one Our Father, three Hail Marys, and one Glory Be. Five decades follow; each decade begins with the Our Father and is followed by ten Hail Marys and one Glory Be.

It is the custom to meditate on the "mysteries" of the life of Jesus and Mary while praying the Rosary. There are three traditional groupings. Also giving the days of the week for when each grouping is to be prayed is just a suggestion and is meant largely for those who pray the Rosary daily.

The Joyful Mysteries
(prayed usually on Mondays, Thursdays, and Saturdays, and may be prayed on Sundays during Advent and Christmas)

1. The Annunciation
2. The Visitation
3. The Nativity
4. The Presentation
5. The Finding of Jesus in the Temple

The Sorrowful Mysteries
(prayed usually on Wednesdays and Fridays)

1. The Agony in the Garden
2. The Scourging at the Pillar
3. The Crowning with Thorns
4. The Carrying of the Cross
5. The Crucifixion

The Glorious Mysteries
(prayed usually on Tuesdays and Sundays)

1. The Resurrection
2. The Ascension
3. The Descent of the Holy Spirit upon the Apostles
4. The Assumption of the Blessed Virgin Mary
5. The Coronation of the Blessed Virgin Mary

In 2002 Pope John Paul added a fourth grouping of mysteries.

The Luminous Mysteries
(prayed usually on Thursdays)

1. The Baptism in the Jordan
2. The Wedding at Cana
3. Proclamation of the Kingdom
4. The Transfiguration
5. Institution of the Eucharist

The Salve Regina

Hail, Holy Queen, Mother of mercy!
Hail, our life, our sweetness, and our hope!

To thee do we cry, poor banished children of Eve.
To thee do we send up our sighs,
mourning and weeping in this valley of tears.
Turn then, most gracious Advocate,
thine eyes of mercy toward us,
and after this, our exile,
show unto us the blessed fruit of thy womb, Jesus
O clement, O loving, O sweet Virgin Mary!

The Angelus

(Usually said at 6 a.m., noon, and 6 p.m. daily, except during the Easter season)

V. The angel of the Lord declared unto Mary.
R. And she conceived of the Holy Spirit.

Hail Mary,…

V. Behold the handmaid of the Lord.
R. Let it be done unto me according to thy word.

Hail Mary,…

V. And the Word was made flesh
R. And dwelt among us.

Hail Mary,…

V. Pray for us, O holy Mother of God
R. That we may be made worthy of the promises of
   Christ

Let us pray: Pour forth, we beseech thee, O Lord,
thy grace into our hearts,
that we, to whom the incarnation of Christ thy Son
was made known by the message of an angel,
may, by his passion and cross,
be brought to the glory of his resurrection
Through the same Christ, Our Lord.
Amen.

The Regina Caeli

(Said in place of the Angelus during the Easter Season)

Rejoice, O Queen of Heaven, Alleluia!
For he whom thou didst merit to bear, Alleluia!
Has risen as he said, Alleluia!
Pray for us to God, Alleluia!

V. Rejoice and be glad, O Virgin Mary, Alleluia!
R. For the Lord has risen indeed, Alleluia!

Let us pray: O God, who hast given joy to the whole
    world
through the resurrection of thy Son, our Lord Jesus
    Christ,
grant that through the prayers of his Virgin Mother
    Mary,
we may obtain the joys of everlasting life.
Through the same Christ, our Lord.
Amen.

The Memorare

Remember, O most gracious Virgin Mary,
that never was it known that anyone who fled to
    your protection,
implored your help, or sought your intercession, was
    left unaided.
Inspired then with confidence, I fly unto you,
O Virgin of virgins, my Mother!
To you do I come, before you I stand, sinful and
    sorrowful.
O Mother of the Word Incarnate, despise not my
    petitions,
but in your mercy, hear and answer me.
Amen.

The Ultima

In Latin and English

Ultima in mortis hora,
Filium pro nobis ora,
Bonam mortem impetra,
Virgo, Mater, Domina.

When death's hour is then upon us,
To your Son pray that he grant us,
Death, both holy and serene,
Virgin Mary, Mother, Queen.

Litany of Loreto, or, Litany of the Blessed Virgin Mary

Lord, have mercy on us. *Christ have mercy on us.*
Lord, have mercy on us.
Christ, hear us. *Christ, graciously hear us.*
God, the Father of heaven, *have mercy on us.*
God the Son, Redeemer of the world, *have mercy on us.*
God the Holy Spirit, *have mercy on us.*
Holy Trinity, one God, *have mercy on us.*

Holy Mary, *pray for us.*
Holy Mother of God, *pray for us.*
Holy Virgin of virgins, *pray for us.*

Mother of Christ, *pray for us.*
Mother of the Church, *pray for us.*
Mother of divine grace, *pray for us.*
Mother most pure, *pray for us.*
Mother most chaste, *pray for us.*
Mother inviolate, *pray for us.*
Mother undefiled, *pray for us.*
Mother most amiable, *pray for us.*
Mother most admirable, *pray for us.*
Mother of good counsel, *pray for us.*
Mother of our Creator, *pray for us.*
Mother of our Savior, *pray for us.*

Virgin most prudent, *pray for us.*
Virgin most venerable, *pray for us.*
Virgin most renowned, *pray for us.*
Virgin most powerful, *pray for us.*
Virgin most merciful, *pray for us.*
Virgin most faithful, *pray for us.*

Mirror of justice, *pray for us.*
Seat of wisdom, *pray for us.*
Cause of our joy, *pray for us.*
Spiritual vessel, *pray for us.*
Vessel of honor, *pray for us.*
Singular vessel of devotion, *pray for us.*
Mystical rose, *pray for us.*
Tower of David, *pray for us.*
Tower of ivory, *pray for us.*
House of gold, *pray for us.*
Ark of the covenant, *pray for us.*
Gate of heaven, *pray for us.*
Morning star, *pray for us.*
Health of the sick, *pray for us.*
Refuge of sinners, *pray for us.*
Comforter of the afflicted, *pray for us.*
Help of Christians, *pray for us.*

Queen of Angels, *pray for us.*
Queen of Patriarchs, *pray for us.*
Queen of Prophets, *pray for us.*
Queen of Apostles, *pray for us.*
Queen of Martyrs, *pray for us.*
Queen of Confessors, *pray for us.*
Queen of Virgins, *pray for us.*
Queen of all Saints, *pray for us.*
Queen conceived without original sin, *pray for us.*
Queen assumed into heaven, *pray for us.*
Queen of the most holy Rosary, *pray for us.*
Queen of the Family, *pray for us.*
Queen of Peace, *pray for us.*

Lamb of God, who takes away the sins of the world, *spare us, O Lord.*

Lamb of God, who takes away the sins of the world, *graciously hear us, O Lord.*

Lamb of God, who takes away the sins of the world, *have mercy on us.*

V. Pray for us, O holy Mother of God
R. That we may be made worthy of the promises of Christ.

Let Us Pray

Grant, we beseech thee, O Lord God, unto us thy servants, that we may rejoice in continual health of mind and body; and, by the glorious intercession of Blessed Mary ever Virgin, may be delivered from present sadness, and enter into the joy of thy eternal gladness. Through Christ our Lord.
Amen.

PRAYER PROMPTS AND EXAMPLES

The United States Conference of Catholic Bishops provides an enormously helpful website (http://www.usccb.org) that features the Scripture readings and psalm for every day of the year, as well as the complete text of *The New American Bible*. This is a rich source for prayerful inspiration. Below are some examples of reflections and prayers inspired by the daily Scriptures, offered with the hope that the reader will make daily use of Scripture in crafting personal prayers to God in supplication, praise, and thanksgiving.

When I am confused about my obligations

Reading: Matthew 1:16–24

Reflection

If St. Joseph had had a corner of his carpentry shop where he sold souvenirs and novelties, he might have had a rack of posters and bumper stickers, one of which would have read: "Bloom where you are planted." That certainly is what Joseph did. Imagine his chagrin and confusion as Mary attempted to explain to him that she was pregnant "through the Holy Spirit." Joseph was an upright man who did not want to expose Mary to the shame attached in their society to pregnancy outside marriage. But until he heard the command of God's angel in his dream, he intended to separate himself from what seemed an unsavory situation at best.

Sometimes we may need a change of venue, a fresh start in a new place. Sometimes we are where we belong and need to be and need instead a fresh attitude. Our prayer at such times should speak to us of peace and the search for peace, of attention to duty with cheerful resignation, and of the joy we seek in life that is for us an infallible sign of the presence of God in our days and our deeds.

Prayer

Father of our Lord Jesus Christ,
you entrusted the care of the boy Jesus, born of the
    Virgin Mary,
to Joseph her husband.
May we, like him, be attentive to your voice and
    your will
even in our confusion and uncertainty.

May we serve you in all that we do
as we make our way through the difficulties of life
on our way to you.
We ask this favor through Christ, our Lord.
Amen.

When I am feeling selfish

When I do not feel generous, the Apostle Paul reminds me: "Whoever sows sparingly will also reap sparingly." In my generous moments, however, he assures me that "whoever sows bountifully will also reap bountifully." We move on with the realization that "God loves a cheerful giver" (2 Cor 9:6, 7). But we can surmise that God also accepts from grumps. In anticipation of God making every grace abundant for us, we move to prayer.

Prayer
Thanks be to you, God, for your indescribable gifts.
You are aware of all our needs and are attentive to
    me
when I feel small and frightened to share.
Assure me that in acknowledging my dependence on
    you,
seeking bread and guidance day by day,
you will always give all that I need
that I might have an abundance for every good work.
Create in me a generous heart,
quicken me in your good Spirit,
and encourage me with a vision of what lies beyond
    my sight
through Christ our Lord.
Amen!

Ash Wednesday

Reading I: Joel 2:12–18
Responsorial Psalm: Ps 51:3–4, 5–6ab, 12–13, 14, and 17
Reading II: 2 Corinthians 5:20—6:2
Gospel: Matthew 6:1–6, 16–18

Reflection

There is something quite curious about our entry into Lent. We hear Jesus say, "When you fast, do not look gloomy like the hypocrites." He tells us, "Anoint your head and wash your face, so that you may not appear to be fasting." But no sooner do we hear that than we bless ashes "by which we show that we are dust" (the Blessing of Ashes) and present our foreheads to be marked with them.

Joel reminds us to "rend your hearts, not your garments," and in this way "return to the Lord, your God. For gracious and merciful is he, slow to anger, rich in kindness, and relenting in punishment." The ashes remind us, "Come back to the Lord with all your heart; leave the past in ashes, and turn to God with tears and fasting, for he is slow to anger and ready to forgive" (Antiphon I, see Joel 2:13).

Jesus, in Matthew's Gospel, points to three paths back to God: almsgiving, prayer, and fasting. Doing those things, we pray more confidently with the psalmist his great lament: "Have mercy on me, O God, in your goodness; in your abundant compassion blot out my offense." Living the life of Jesus by imitating him in our thoughts, words, and deeds, we come to the secret of the season in one of the next verses of the psalm: "Restore my joy in your salvation; sustain in me a willing spirit."

Most people do not associate Lenten penance with joy, but to do so is clearly the mind of the Church as the first

Preface of Lent reveals: "Each year you give us this joyful season / when we prepare to celebrate the paschal mystery / with mind and heart renewed."

We brush aside the ashes and hasten into the Lenten days with clean faces, knowing that through works of charity and self-sacrifice, we will prepare ourselves to renew our baptismal promises and enter the Easter feast with a keen awareness of our own dignity as baptized sons and daughters of God, committed, in cooperation with the Holy Spirit, to renewing the earth.

The Apostle Paul helps us to begin this Lenten journey:

> Working together, then,
> we appeal to you not to receive the grace of God in vain.
> For he says:
> "In an acceptable time I heard you,
> and on the day of salvation I helped you."
> Behold, now is a very acceptable time;
> behold, now is the day of salvation. (2 Cor 6:1–2)

Prayer
> Almighty God,
> as we begin our Lenten journey,
> we ask you to make these days holy and joyful
> that we may conquer our sinfulness,
> leave the past in ashes,
> and in our care for our sisters and brothers,
> come to know the promise of your salvation
> which is revealed and bestowed
> in the death and resurrection of Jesus Christ,
> your Son and our Lord,
> through whom we pray to you, our One God
> in the unity of the Holy Spirit.
> Amen.

Wednesday in the Octave of Easter

Reading I: Acts 3:1–10
Responsorial Psalm: Psalm 105:1–2, 3–4, 6–7, 8–9
Gospel: Luke 24:13–35

Reflection

The road to Emmaus provides a model for the Church's liturgy: greeting, Liturgy of the Word, homily, table prayer, sharing of the blessed bread and wine, recognition of the Lord in our midst and at our table.

Why did the disciples not recognize Jesus? Luke tells us that Jesus drew near to them and walked with them, but that they were somehow prevented from recognizing him. Luke seems to provide a hint why they did not recognize him; we see the hint in the verb tense as they reported that "we were hoping" that he would be the one to redeem Israel. As they tell the story of Jesus and their hopes, they use the past tense. Their hope is gone. They disclose that some women from their group astounded them by reporting that they were at the tomb early in the morning, but did not find his body. Instead, they claimed to have seen a vision of angels who announced that he was alive. Others, presumably the men, went then to the tomb and found things there just as the women had described, but they did not see Jesus.

When the disciples recognize Christ in the breaking of the bread, they learn that the Church never speaks of the Risen Lord in the past tense. When the liturgy was first translated into English, the first memorial acclamation was incorrectly rendered as "Christ has died, Christ has risen, Christ will come again." "Has risen" was quickly changed to the more accurate "is risen." This Christ is always present to the Church in the present tense and not just as a sweet memory.

Prayer
>Almighty God,
>our companion and guide,
>Be present to each of us and to all your Church
>That we may always know and celebrate the fullness
>of the death and resurrection of Jesus Christ,
>your Son and our Lord,
>through whom we pray to you, our One God
>in the unity of the Holy Spirit.
>Amen.

Wednesday of the Second Week of Easter

Reading I: Acts 5:17–26
Responsorial Psalm: Psalm 34:2–3, 4–5, 6–7, 8–9
Gospel: John 3:16–21

Reflection

In Sunday school, children sometimes carefully copy John 3:16 in their very best script: "God so loved the world that he gave his only Son, / so that everyone who believes in him might not perish / but might have eternal life." Taking a walnut, they remove the meat, and insert the carefully folded verse. They glue the walnut back together, paint it gold, and adorn it with precious beads or bits of glass. They then have the gospel in a nutshell.

God has given a great gift, but John the Gospel writer laments "that the light came into the world, / but people preferred darkness to light." It must not be that way with those who seek the truth. The Opening Prayer for today's liturgy reminds us that God has filled us with the hope of resurrection by restoring us to our original dignity. We hear often of original sin; this prayer, made in the radiance of

Easter light, points us to our original dignity. We continue to pray that we who relive this mystery each year might come to share it in perpetual love.

Ours is a grand vision and a great hope. Easter fuels both, and prompts us, rejoicing, to remember that "God did not send his Son into the world to condemn the world, / but that the world might be saved through him."

Prayer

Almighty God,
who sent your Word for our salvation,
restore us,
keep us in your light that never diminishes,
and teach us to love you and one another better.
We ask this through our Lord Jesus Christ,
in the unity of the Holy Spirit.
Amen.

NOTES AND
FURTHER READING

Some of the chapters in this book include snippets, rewrites, or edited versions from articles or chapters of books I have written earlier; in each case, I am the copyright holder. Unless otherwise indicated, the prayers, rituals, and exercises throughout the book are my own.

The availability of Web resources is amazing. Those who are generous enough to make available classics from our tradition for our free use are certainly thanked and our promised prayers are offered in gratitude. The addresses for online sources are accurate as of this printing, but because Web resources are often moved, taken down, or changed, any item that is not in the reported spot can usually be found by employing one of the number of Web search engines, which are both plentiful and free.

Here are key Web sites of extraordinary value to Catholics:

The Vatican's home page is among the most amazing of resources:
http://www.vatican.va/

The documents of the Second Vatican Council can be found at the Vatican site in a variety of languages at:
http://www.vatican.va/archive/hist_councils/ii_vatican
_council/

The *Catechism of the Catholic Church* is also available at
the Vatican site at:
http://www.vatican.va/archive/ccc/index.htm

The United States Conference of Catholic Bishops provides
on their Web site an enormously generous and helpful
set of resources, including an index of the Church's
social teachings, readings for daily Mass, and a rich collection of other references. The main Web address is at:
http://www.usccb.org/

The online version of *The New American Bible*, book by
book, verse by verse, is on the bishops' site at:
http://www.usccb.org/nab/bible/

The readings for each day's celebration of the Eucharist are at:
http://www.usccb.org/nab/

Introduction

The monk Boso's comment to Anselm was cited by Berard
Marthaler in *The Creed: The Apostolic Faith in
Contemporary Theology*, revised edition (Mystic, CT:
Twenty-Third Publications, 1993), 96.

Chapter 1. The Big Picture: Structure, Governance, and Issues

St. Cyril of Jerusalem's catechetical instruction can be found
online at a number of sites, including:
http://www.crossroadsinitiative.com/library_article/
494/Jerusalem_Catecheses_1_12_Cyril_of_Jerusalem.
html

The Imitation of Christ by Thomas à Kempis is a spiritual classic; it can be found at:
http://www.catholicfirst.com/thefaith/catholicclassics/tkempis/iofchrist.cfm

The *Code of Canon Law* can be found at:
http://www.vatican.va/archive/ENG1104/_INDEX.HTM
The paragraphs and sentences are numbered for easy reference, as in this example: (#386 §1).

The *General Norms for the Liturgical Year and the Calendar* can be found at:
http://www.liturgyoffice.org.uk/Calendar/Info/GNLY.pdf

Pope John Paul II's book *Crossing the Threshold of Hope* (New York: Knopf, 1995) is valuable reading.

Dominus Iesus, "The declaration on the unicity and salvific universality of Jesus Christ and the Church" is available at:
http://www.vatican.va/roman_curia/congregations/cfaith/documents/rc_con_cfaith_doc_20000806_dominus-iesus_en.html

Chapter 2. The Local View: Structures and Tools

The Letter of St. Ignatius of Antioch to the Romans is widely available online, including at:
http://www.newadvent.org/fathers/0107.htm

The Springs of Contemplation: A Retreat at the Abbey of Gethsemani by Thomas Merton (Notre Dame, IN: Ave Maria Press, 1996) is a particularly good read during Holy Week and the Easter season.

The *Missa de Angelis*, Mass VIII, can sometimes be found online, and in a number of hymnals, including the *Liber Usualis* by the Monks of the Abbey of Solemnes. It's available at: http://www.musicasacra.com/2007/07/17/liber-usualis-online/

Chapter 3. Sacraments: Faith, Religion, and Theology in Practice

St. Basil the Great's treatise *On the Holy Spirit* is accessible at: http://www.st-philip.net/presentations/On_the_Holy_Spirit.pdf

On Prayer by Karl Rahner (New York: Paulist Press, 1968) is a small and helpful resource, just 109 pages. It is out of print, but used copies can be located online.

Parts of *Sermons and Discourses: 1839–1857* by John Henry Cardinal Newman can be found online. This site may be helpful: http://www.newmanreader.org/controversies/guides/favorites.html

The quotations from St. Basil the Great and Theophane the Recluse can be found in *Ordinary Graces: Christian Teachings on the Interior Life*, edited by Lorraine Kisly (New York: Bell Tower, 2000), pages 196 and 82 respectively.

The early Christian document entitled *Shepherd of Hermas* is available at: http://www.earlychristianwritings.com/shepherd.html

An excerpt from *The Catecheses*, by John Chrysostom, can be found at:
http://www.crossroadsinitiative.com/library_article/106/Moses_and_Christ_St._John_Chrysostom.html

The Rites of the Catholic Church is in two volumes; the third edition was published by the Liturgical Press in 1990; it is a rich reference for study of and meditation on the prayers and rituals of the Church.

"On the Care for the Dead," a treastise by St. Augustine, can be found at:
http://www.arts.cornell.edu/Classics/faculty/EREbillard_files/rebillard_commemoration.pdf

Chapter 4. But, Then, What About ...?

The nativity homily by Leo the Great can be found at:
http://www.orthodox.net/nativity/nativity-leo-1.html

Chapter 6. Contemporary Challenges

Gregory of Nyssa's treatise on *Christian Perfection*, as well as others of his, can be found at:
http://www.ccel.org/ccel/schaff/npnf205.ix.ii.i.html

The anonymous *Letter to Diognetus* is available at:
http://www.ccel.org/ccel/richardson/fathers.x.i.ii.html

The encyclicals of John Paul II with study tools can be found at:
http://www.vatican.va/holy_father/john_paul_ii/encyclicals/index.htm

The 1991 pastoral letter "Renewing the Earth: An Invitation to Reflection and Action on Environment in Light of Catholic Social Teaching," by the bishops of the United States, can be found at: http://www.usccb.org/sdwp/ejp/bishopsstatement.shtml

The 1975 *Declaration on Certain Questions Concerning Sexual Ethics (Persona humana)* is accessible at: http://www.vatican.va/roman_curia/congregations/cfaith/documents/rc_con_cfaith_doc_19751229_persona-humana_en.html

See *Confronting Power and Sex in the Catholic Church: Reclaiming the Spirit of Jesus* by Bishop Geoffrey Robinson (Collegeville, MN: Liturgical Press, 2008).

See also *Clericalism: The Death of Priesthood* by George B. Wilson (Collegeville, MN: Liturgical Press, 2008).